Contents

Chapter 1
Rebrand YOU using Dermal Fillers, Botulinum
Neurotoxins, and Permanent Cosmetics   11

Chapter 2
The Pre-work for Masterminding the Femme Fatale
Metamorphosis Effect in YOU   21

Chapter 3
The Evolution of Male Aesthetics Using Botulinum
Neurotoxins, Dermal Fillers, and Permanent Eyebrow
Makeup   34

Chapter 4
Decoding the Perfect Timing to Explore Non-Invasive
Cosmetic Treatments   43

Chapter 5
The Benefits of Exclusivity in the Privileged Realm of
Concierge Beauty Services   50

Chapter 6
Elevate Your Social Gathering by Hosting a Cosmetic
Injection Party with Botulinum Neurotoxins and Dermal
Fillers   59

Chapter 7
Selecting Your Perfect Practitioner: Choosing the Right
Match   62

Chapter 8
The Virtual Aesthetic Experience: Modernizing
Consultations for Ease and Efficiency   67

Chapter 9
Understanding the Benefits of Botulinum Neurotoxin
Treatments   71

Chapter 10
Facial Contouring and Volume Restoration using Dermal
Fillers   85

Chapter 11
What is Permanent Makeup: Eyebrows, Lips Blushing, and
Cheek Blushing   96

Conclusion   116

Dedication

This book is a tribute to all those who boldly embark on the journey of The Femme Fatale Metamorphosis Effect.

To you—the brave souls who venture into the depths of self-discovery, embracing both triumphs and trials—I dedicate these pages. May they serve as a guiding light, illuminating your path and revealing the power within you to embark on the transformative journey of the Femme Fatale Metamorphosis Effect.

May you be inspired to embrace your innate authority, delving deep within to create your own unique vision of beauty and strength, both inwardly and outwardly.

This dedication is extended to those who face adversity with resilience, find solace in creative self-expression, and relentlessly pursue authenticity and fulfillment.

May your journey be adorned with moments of enlightenment, growth, and joy. And always remember, true beauty lies not in perfection, but in the courage to embrace your true self.

With Respect and Admiration,

Love Always,

"Andi" Andrea Marie Wady – Bachelor of Science in Healthcare Administration, Life Coach, Licensed Esthetician, Cosmetic Injector, Micropigmentation Practitioner, Custom Formulation and Private Label Brand Consultant, Cosmeceutical Formulator, Educator, Author, Speaker, and Founder of AERDNA EIRAM a division of Redefine Injection Concierges Inc.

THE FEMME FATALE METAMORPHOSIS EFFECT

A Guide to Empowerment and Rebranding Your Identity by Redefining Your Persona with Non-Invasive Cosmetic Procedures

"Andi" Andrea Marie Wady
BSHA, LC, LE, CI, MPS

About the Author

I am "Andi" Andrea Marie Wady, a proud Texan from Longview and raised in Houston. My journey has been a turbulent ride of self-discovery, marked by triumphs and setbacks alike. Yet, each stumble along the way has served as a stepping stone toward understanding myself better.

My earliest recollection of self-awareness dates back to the age of 5. In 1984, the world seemed unprepared for a little black girl like me, with distinctive features – big lips, red hair, freckles, and bursting with energy. Enduring relentless bullying in elementary school was unfortunately, the norm, but it only strengthened my resolve to persevere. By the time I entered middle school, my passion for aesthetics blossomed. Makeup became my refuge, allowing me to conceal freckles and reduce the appearance of my lips, while dark brown hair dye became my faithful companion in masking my natural red afro. Through these small transformations, I found solace in expressing

myself, even if underneath the surface, a lingering sense of insecurity persisted.

Upon becoming a mother at the age of 26, I came to the profound realization that merely employing superficial remedies to soothe my internal insecurities no longer sufficed for the profound lessons I aspired to impart upon my daughter. Seeking deeper meaning, I embarked on a spiritual journey, immersing myself in spirituality, sacred texts, self-help literature, and the cosmic wisdom of astrology. I soon realized that true transformation transcends superficial changes; it requires delving into the depths of one's psyche and spirit to unravel its mysteries.

With this newfound understanding guiding me, I pursued diverse careers in K-12 education, collegiate education, management, consulting, and entrepreneurship, ranging from healthcare and medical aesthetics. Each endeavor became a thread woven into the fabric of my quest for self-discovery and empowerment.

Though I initially followed career paths that didn't fully align with my teenage infatuation, I never lost sight of those aspirations. The second phase of my pursuit of formal knowledge commenced in 2012 upon the attainment of my Life Coach Certification from the American University of NLP. A Few years later in 2015, at the age of 36, I finally took a leap of faith and began my medical aesthetics educational journey. I returned to school earning a Non-Invasive Advanced Body Contouring and Skin Tightening Certification from the Texas Laser Institute. Building upon that foundation, in 2016 I graduated from Ogle School and obtained my Esthetician License, further augmenting my skills with certifications in Diseases of the Skin and Cosmeceutical Products from the International Dermal Institute.

Driven by an insatiable thirst for knowledge, I underwent rigorous training in Permanent Makeup in 2015 and became a Micropigmentation Specialist. In 2023, I incorporated my company, AERDNA EIRAM, a division of Redefine Injection Concierges Inc., and pursued additional certifications in Advanced Comprehensive Hands-On Techniques on All Botulinum Neurotoxins from MySpaLive, culminating in certifications as a Master Neurotoxin Practitioner, Expert Lip Filler Specialist, and Master Chin and Cheek Filler Technician from Master Injectors Inc. These achievements, and a few more, coupled with my B.S. in Healthcare Administration, represent my mastery in the field of Medical Aesthetics where I seamlessly blend my passion for Esthetics with a commitment to Healthcare, Education, and Business.

Preface

Have you ever felt drawn to explore the transformative potential that resides within you, but uncertain about how to birth it into reality?

The Femme Fatale Metamorphosis Effect also known as the FFM Effect or FFME is not just a concept that I conceived; it is a profound awakening to the essence of marrying self-realization, personal empowerment, and self-image together into the physical manifestation of your ideal self.

It is a journey that transcends age, defying societal norms and expectations, and embracing the true inner and outer essence of your evolved womanhood.

Imagine a world where a woman steps into her own light, shedding the layers of self-doubt and societal conditioning to reveal her authentic self. This metamorphosis is not merely about physical appearance but a deep inner shift that radiates confidence, strength, and resilience. It is about rewriting the narrative of one's life, embracing the wisdom and grace that come with age, and celebrating the beauty of experience and self-discovery.

As we navigate the complexities of life, especially in our 40s and beyond, it becomes crucial to redefine our sense of self and purpose as it aligns with our consciousness. The Femme Fatale Metamorphosis Effect offers a pathway to reinvention, a journey of self-discovery that empowers women to embrace their true potential and live life on their own terms. It is about stepping into the fullness of who we are, unapologetically and fiercely, with a newfound sense of liberation and empowerment.

While this journey may not be a one-size-fits-all solution, its impact can be profound and life-changing. It is a testament to the resilience of the human spirit and the power of self-belief. Through seeking support, whether through therapy, mentorship, or self-reflection, women can unlock the limitless potential that resides within them and embark on a transformative journey toward self-actualization.

So, dear woman, embrace the empowered being within you, for the Femme Fatale Metamorphosis Effect beckons you to unleash your inner strength, beauty, and wisdom. It is a journey of self-transformation that knows no bounds, inviting you to rewrite your story, reclaim your power, and shine brightly as the radiant woman you are meant to be inside and out.

Chapter 1

Rebrand YOU using Dermal Fillers, Botulinum Neurotoxins, and Permanent Cosmetics

The journey towards self-discovery and authenticity takes center stage in a world that places a premium on image and self-expression. It's not just about appearances; it's about unveiling your inner essence and projecting it outwardly with confidence and grace. Embracing one's true self involves honoring and enhancing unique features in a way that aligns with personal ideals of beauty. Enter the realm of non-invasive cosmetic procedures – where Botulinum Neurotoxins, Dermal Fillers, and Permanent Makeup act as tools of transformation, empowering individuals to redefine their image while staying true to themselves. This chapter delves into the profound impact of authenticity on flawless personal rebranding using non-invasive cosmetic procedures.

The Power of Authenticity

At the core of every successful transformation lies authenticity – the bedrock of self-expression and self-assurance. It's about recognizing and embracing your unique quirks, flaws, and strengths, and weaving them into a tapestry that reflects your true self. Authenticity is not about conforming to societal standards but about celebrating your individuality and letting your inner light shine through.

Key Pillars of Authenticity

·   **Self-Discovery:** Dive deep into your inner world to uncover your true essence and values.

·   **Self-Acceptance:** Embrace your imperfections as part of your beauty, for they are what make you one-of-a-kind.

·   **Self-Expression:** Let your personality and beliefs guide your outward appearance, creating a seamless fusion of inner and outer beauty.

Rebrand Your Identity with Cosmetic Enhancements

Cosmetic procedures like Botulinum Neurotoxins, Dermal Fillers, and Permanent Makeup serve as catalysts for self-expression and enhancement, elevating your natural beauty to new heights. When embraced authentically, these treatments can accentuate your features while preserving your uniqueness and individuality.

1. Botulinum Neurotoxins

·   Smooth away fine lines and wrinkles to reveal a more relaxed and rejuvenated version of yourself.

·   Boost your confidence by addressing areas of concern, allowing your inner radiance to shine through.

·   Achieve natural-looking results that enhance your facial expressions without compromising your authenticity.

2. Dermal Fillers

·   Restore lost volume in key areas like the chin, cheeks, and lips, enhancing facial contours and symmetry.

·   Rejuvenate your appearance by minimizing wrinkles and creating a vibrant, youthful look that mirrors your inner vitality.

·   Tailor your treatment to your unique needs and aesthetic goals, ensuring a personalized approach that honors your natural beauty.

3. Permanent Makeup

·   Effortless Beauty: Permanent Makeup allows you to wake up feeling polished and confident, without the need for daily touch-ups. By enhancing your features in a natural and understated way, you can streamline your daily routine and embrace your true self.

·   Time-Saving Convenience: Say goodbye to the hassle of applying makeup every day. With Permanent Makeup, you can enjoy long-lasting results that free up time for other pursuits. Whether you're a busy professional or a busy parent, this beauty solution can help you look your best with minimal effort.

·   Subtle Enhancement: Permanent Makeup is all about enhancing your natural beauty while maintaining a subtle and refined appearance. By working with a qualified practitioner, you can achieve results that enhance your unique features and reflect your individuality.

Break Free by Overcoming a Self-Limiting Mindset

In the journey towards realizing our dreams and aspirations, one of the biggest obstacles we face is our own self-limiting beliefs. These beliefs, entrenched in our minds, whisper doubts about our capabilities and worthiness, hindering us from reaching our full potential. However, by recognizing, challenging, and transcending these mental barriers, we can pave the way for boundless growth and success.

Identifying self-limiting beliefs is the first step towards liberation. It requires introspection and self-awareness to pinpoint the negative narratives that have taken root in our psyche. Whether it's the fear of failure, feelings of inadequacy, or ingrained notions of unworthiness, acknowledging these limitations is crucial in dismantling their hold over us.

Confronting self-limiting beliefs demands courage and resilience. It involves challenging the validity of these beliefs and reframing our mindset towards empowerment and possibility. By questioning the narratives that confine us and replacing them with affirming thoughts, we can gradually weaken the grip of self-doubt and insecurity.

Outgrowing a self-limiting mindset is a transformative process that necessitates perseverance and commitment. It involves cultivating a mindset of abundance, self-belief, and resilience in the face of challenges. By embracing growth-oriented attitudes and focusing on our strengths and potential, we can expand our horizons and unlock new possibilities we once deemed unattainable.

Transcending self-limiting beliefs is a liberating journey that empowers us to embrace our true potential. By shedding the shackles of doubt and fear, we pave the way for personal growth, fulfillment, and success. So, let us embark on this transformative path with courage, conviction, and a steadfast belief in our ability to soar beyond limitations and soar toward our aspirations.

Understanding Self-Limiting Beliefs

Do you ever feel like you're your own worst enemy, holding yourself back from reaching your true potential? Self-limiting beliefs are the invisible barriers that we construct within our minds, hindering our growth and success. These beliefs often originate from past experiences, societal pressures, or internal anxieties. Identifying and overcoming them is key to unlocking your full capabilities.

Imposter Syndrome is a common self-limiting belief that plagues many individuals. It manifests as a constant fear of being exposed as a fraud, despite your accomplishments and capabilities. The fear of failure is another insidious belief that can paralyze us, preventing us from seizing new opportunities or taking on challenges. Embracing imperfection is essential in combating perfectionism, a belief that demands flawless execution and often leads to procrastination and avoidance.

Negative self-talk, the silent but powerful voice that feeds our doubts and insecurities, is yet another hurdle to conquer. By recognizing these self-limiting beliefs and reframing our perspectives, we can break free from their constraints and move towards self-empowerment.

Shedding these self-imposed limitations requires a shift in mindset and a commitment to self-growth. Embrace your strengths and weaknesses, celebrate your accomplishments, and learn from your failures. Surround yourself with positivity and support and challenge yourself to step outside your comfort zone.

Remember, you can achieve greatness once you release yourself from the shackles of self-doubt. Break free from the confines of self-limiting beliefs and pave the way for a future filled with endless possibilities.

3 Steps to Recognizing and Overcoming Self-Limiting Beliefs

Shifting from a self-limiting mindset to one of empowerment begins with acknowledging and understanding the beliefs that hinder your personal growth. Here are effective techniques to uncover and address these limiting beliefs:

1. Embrace Self-Reflection

·   **Journaling:** Dedicate time to writing down your thoughts, emotions, and experiences. By reviewing your journal entries, you can pinpoint recurring negative beliefs that may be holding you back.

·   **Practicing Mindfulness:** Engage in mindfulness activities to heighten your awareness of your thought patterns and how they impact your feelings and behaviors.

2. Solicit Feedback

·   **Consult Trusted Individuals:** Seek input from close friends and mentors who can offer an objective perspective on your strengths and weaknesses.

·   **Professional Support:** Consider enlisting the help of a therapist or coach who specializes in identifying and challenging self-limiting beliefs.

3. Recognize Triggers

·   **Situational Cues:** Be attuned to circumstances that trigger self-doubt or negative thoughts. These triggers often lead to the discovery of underlying limiting beliefs.

·   **Emotional Responses:** Monitor your emotional reactions to obstacles or setbacks as they can unveil deep-seated self-limiting beliefs.

By incorporating these strategies into your self-improvement journey, you pave the way for personal growth and a renewed sense of self-awareness. Remember, overcoming self-limiting beliefs is a process that requires patience, persistence, and a willingness to confront and challenge your inner barriers.

Challenging and Reframing Self-Limiting Beliefs into Empowering Truths

The first step towards breaking free from a self-limiting mindset is acknowledging the beliefs that constrain you. Here are effective strategies to help you pinpoint and confront these self-limiting beliefs head-on.

3 Steps to Identifying Triggers and Overcoming Self-Limiting Beliefs

Become attuned to situational triggers and emotional responses that unveil your self-limiting beliefs. By recognizing these cues, you can begin the process of challenging and reframing your self-limiting beliefs.

1. **Interrogate Your Beliefs:** Scrutinize the evidence supporting your self-limiting beliefs. Counter them with instances of past successes and positive feedback to debunk their validity.

2. **Reframe Your Mindset:** Replace negative self-talk with positive affirmations that empower and motivate you. Embrace a growth mindset that thrives on challenges and sees setbacks as opportunities for growth.

3. **Envision Success:** Engage in mental rehearsal by visualizing your triumphs and mapping out the steps towards achieving your goals. Picture your future self,

liberated from self-limiting beliefs, and embody their confidence and resilience.

5 Steps to Taking Bold Actions Towards Transformation

Breaking free from self-limiting beliefs demands proactive steps and a commitment to self-improvement. Embrace challenges, confront your doubts, and take decisive action to build confidence through experience. Remember, your potential knows no bounds once you liberate yourself from the shackles of self-doubt. Embark on this transformative journey today and watch your true capabilities soar to new heights.

Unleash Your Inner Power: Embrace the Femme Fatale Metamorphosis Effect from within

Embarking on a journey of self-transformation requires courage, determination, and a willingness to embrace change. The path to unlocking your true potential toward a Femme Fatale Metamorphosis Effect is paved with challenges and opportunities for growth. By following these 5 key steps, you can tap into your inner power, confidence, and sensuality to become a woman of irresistible charm and influence.

1. **Embrace Your Unique Charisma:** The Femme Fatale Metamorphosis Effect archetype embodies a captivating blend of seduction, mystery, and confidence. Embrace your unique charisma and unleash the magnetic allure that sets you apart from the crowd. Cultivate a sense of self-assurance that radiates from within, drawing others to you like moths to a flame.

2. **Embody Self-Confidence:** Confidence is the cornerstone of the Femme Fatale Metamorphosis Effect persona. Believe in your worth and value, exuding an air of self-assurance that commands attention and respect. Embrace your strengths and imperfections alike, knowing that they contribute to your undeniable allure.

3. **Cultivate Inner Strength:** The Femme Fatale Metamorphosis Effect is a symbol of independence and inner strength. Develop resilience in the face of challenges, learning to bounce back from setbacks with grace and determination. Embrace your vulnerabilities as sources of power, transforming them into strengths that set you apart from the crowd.

4. **Embrace Your Sensuality:** Sensuality is a key element of the Femme Fatale Metamorphosis Effect mystique. Embrace your femininity and sensuality, celebrating the beauty and allure of your physical form. Connect with your desires and passions, allowing them to fuel your journey towards self-discovery and empowerment.

5. **Master the Art of Influence:** The Femme Fatale Metamorphosis Effect wields influence with grace and subtlety, captivating others with her words and actions. Hone your communication skills, learning to convey your thoughts and emotions with confidence and charisma. Cultivate a magnetic presence that leaves a lasting impression on those around you.

By following these steps and embracing the essence of the Femme Fatale Metamorphosis Effect archetype, you can unlock the full potential of your inner power and charisma. Embrace the transformational journey ahead, knowing that you possess the strength, confidence, and allure to become a woman of irresistible charm and influence.

Master the Art of Seduction and Empowerment

In a world where confidence is key and allure is everything, embracing your Femme Fatale Metamorphosis Effect energy can be a game-changer. The Femme Fatale Metamorphosis Effect embodies a unique blend of mystery, intelligence, sensuality, and independence that captivates those around her. Are you ready to step into your power and unleash your inner seductress?

5 Steps to Help You Master Your Femme Fatale Metamorphosis Effect Energy

1. **Embrace Self-Confidence:** Confidence is not just a trait; it's a lifestyle. Start by rewiring your mindset with positive self-talk that affirms your worth and capabilities. Stand tall, make eye contact, and let your body language exude confidence. Remember, self-care is non-negotiable – invest in practices that make you feel good about yourself.

2. **Cultivate an Air of Mystery:** Mystery is the secret ingredient that keeps them coming back for more. Guard your personal life, be a good listener, and master the art of subtlety. Leave others intrigued and wanting to unravel the enigma that is you.

3. **Harness Your Intelligence and Strategy:** Intelligence is sexy, and strategic thinking is your superpower. Stay informed, think ahead, and use your emotional intelligence to navigate social interactions like a pro. Remember, knowledge is not just power – it's magnetic.

4. **Embrace Your Sensuality:** Sensuality is your weapon of choice. Be aware of your body language, dress in a way that makes you feel confident and attractive; and indulge

your senses in experiences that please you. Allow your sensuality to be a force to be reckoned with.

5. **Assert Your Independence:** Independence is the cornerstone of the Femme Fatale Metamorphosis Effect persona. Cultivate self-reliance, set healthy boundaries, and pursue your passions with unwavering determination. Remember, true empowerment comes from within.

Embrace the allure and power of the Femme Fatale Metamorphosis Effect within you and watch as your world transforms around you. By tapping into your inner confidence, mystery, intelligence, sensuality, and independence, you can become a force to be reckoned with. This journey is not about changing who you are, but about unlocking your true potential and radiating irresistible charm and influence.

Chapter 2

The Pre-work for Masterminding the Femme Fatale Metamorphosis Effect in YOU

There exists within every woman a powerful and enigmatic force waiting to be awakened – the essence of the Femme Fatale Metamorphosis Effect. She is seductive, mysterious, and exudes an undeniable confidence that captivates all who encounter her. Embracing this transformative energy is a journey of self-discovery and empowerment, a path toward unlocking the hidden depths of your allure and influence.

To embody the Femme Fatale Metamorphosis Effect is to step into your power with unwavering confidence and grace. It is a metamorphosis that transcends mere appearance, delving deep into the core of your being to unleash a magnetic energy that demands attention and respect. This is not about conforming to external standards of beauty or behavior, but rather about embracing your unique essence and owning it with pride.

The first step towards mastering your Femme Fatale Metamorphosis Effect persona is embracing your inner strength and self-assurance. Believe in the power that resides within you, the power to command attention and influence those around you. Cultivate a mindset of confidence and empowerment, knowing that you are worthy of all the success and admiration that comes your way.

Next, tap into your sensuality – the inherent femininity that sets you apart and makes you truly irresistible. Embrace your curves, your softness, your allure, and let them shine brightly for the world to see. Sensuality is not just about physical attributes, but also about the way you carry yourself, the way you speak, and the way you interact with others. Let your inner sensuality radiate outward, enveloping those around you in the warmth of your presence.

Finally, embody the air of mystery that is synonymous with the Femme Fatale Metamorphosis Effect archetype. Keep them guessing, keep them intrigued, and always leave them wanting more. Cultivate a sense of enigma and allure that draws others towards you like moths to a flame, while maintaining a sense of independence and self-assurance that sets you apart from the crowd.

By embracing the Femme Fatale Metamorphosis Effect, you are stepping into your magic – a magic that is uniquely yours and yours alone. Embrace it, nurture it, and let it guide you toward a life filled with confidence, allure, and influence. Unleash the Femme Fatale Metamorphosis Effect within and watch as the world unfolds at your feet in awe and admiration.

Understanding the Femme Fatale Metamorphosis Effect Archetype

The allure of the Femme Fatale Metamorphosis Effect transcends mere seduction; she is a force to be reckoned with, embodying self-assurance, intellect, and a profound sense of self-worth. This captivating archetype is steeped in a tapestry of cultural and historical narratives, representing independence, resilience, and an enigmatic magnetism that intrigues and captivates all who encounter her.

The Femme Fatale Metamorphosis Effect exudes an aura of empowerment and sophistication, commanding attention with her unwavering confidence and sharp intellect. She navigates the complexities of life with grace and poise, unafraid to challenge societal norms and expectations. Her enigmatic nature draws others in, leaving them spellbound by her mysterious charm and undeniable presence.

The Femme Fatale Metamorphosis Effect stands out as a symbol of strength and autonomy in a world that often seeks to confine women to narrow stereotypes. She defies conventions and embraces her individuality, unapologetically charting her course in a sea of conformity. Her confidence is infectious, inspiring others to embrace their true selves and break free from the constraints of societal expectations.

The legacy of the Femme Fatale Metamorphosis Effect resonates across time and culture, serving as a reminder of the enduring power of female agency and resilience. She is a testament to the limitless potential of women and a beacon of empowerment for those who dare to challenge the status quo. In her, we find a reflection of our inner strength and a reminder that true empowerment comes from embracing our authentic selves without reservation.

So, let us embrace the spirit of the Femme Fatale Metamorphosis Effect harnessing her strength, intelligence, and self-assurance to carve out our paths and rewrite the narratives that seek to define us. Let us revel in the power of our individuality and stand boldly in our truth, unafraid to embrace the mystery and allure that lies within each of us. For in the essence of the Femme Fatale Metamorphosis Effect, we find the key to unlocking our true potential and embracing the fullness of who we are meant to be.

Unveil Your Inner Goddess: 4 Qualities That Define a Woman of Power

In a world where strength and grace intertwine, a woman of power stands tall, captivating those around her with an aura of confidence that radiates from within.

1. She is the embodiment of mystery, holding back just enough to keep others intrigued, always leaving them wanting more.

2. Her intelligence is a weapon, sharp and strategic, guiding her every move with precision and purpose. But it's her sensuality that truly sets her apart.

3. She understands the allure of her femininity, embracing it without reservation, and using it as a source of power to command attention and respect.

4.   She knows that her independence is her greatest asset, standing firm in her self-reliance, and never seeking validation from others.

To embody these qualities is to embrace the essence of a goddess, a woman who knows her worth, her strength, and her allure. So, step into your power, unleash your inner goddess, and let the world see the true magic that lies within you.

4 Tips to Master Your Femme Fatale Metamorphosis Effect Energy

1.   Unleashing Your Inner Radiance: Confidence is not just a trait but a way of life that empowers the essence of your being.

2.   Believe in Your Brilliance: Let go of self-doubts and embrace a mindset that champions your unique talents and capabilities. Every thought should be a melody of self-affirmation that resonates with your inner brilliance.

3.   Embody Your Strength: Stand tall like a beacon of light, let your eyes mirror the depth of your soul, and let your gestures speak a language of power. Your very presence should be a tapestry woven with threads of confidence.

4.   Nurture Your Essence: Dedicate moments to self-care rituals that nurture your mind, body, and spirit. Whether it's indulging in a skincare routine that illuminates your skin, engaging in physical activities that invigorate your body, or meditating to find peace within, each practice should be a celebration of your essence.

Remember, confidence is not a destination but a journey of

self-discovery and empowerment. Embrace your inner radiance, for it is the light that guides you to your true potential.

3 Tips to Cultivate an Air of Mystery

A captivating persona is shrouded in an enigma in the art of allure. To exude an air of mystery that intrigues and captivates, consider the following keys:

1. **Embrace Discretion**: Choose what to reveal about yourself judiciously, weaving a tapestry of intrigue with selective glimpses into your world.

2. **Master the Art of Listening:** Engage in conversations with a genuine curiosity for others, allowing them to take center stage while you unveil the beauty of silence and attentive understanding.

3. **Embrace Subtlety:** Like a hidden gem waiting to be discovered, sprinkle subtle hints and gestures that hint at depths unseen, leaving a trail of curiosity in your wake.

In the dance of charm and mystery, the allure lies not in what is shown but in what is left to the imagination. Embrace the power of the unknown and watch as fascination and curiosity blossom in your wake.

3 Tips to Harness Your Intelligence and Strategy

Unlocking the essence of the Femme Fatale Metamorphosis Effect metamorphosis goes beyond traditional stereotypes; it's about embodying intelligence and strategic prowess in everything you do. As you embark on this empowering journey, remember these key principles:

1. **The Pursuit of Knowledge:** A Femme Fatale Metamorphosis Effect is a perpetual learner, constantly seeking to expand her wisdom across various domains. Embracing the power of continuous learning, for intelligence, is not only captivating but also a fundamental element of allure.

2. **Strategic Brilliance:** Every move you make should be intentional and calculated. Cultivate your strategic thinking skills, envisioning your path forward and meticulously planning your next steps. By doing so, you seize control of your narrative and shape your destiny with purpose.

3. **Harnessing Emotional Intelligence:** Your emotional landscape is a treasure trove waiting to be explored. Dive deep into the realm of emotional intelligence, understanding and mastering your feelings. By harnessing your emotional awareness, you gain the ability to navigate social complexities with grace and finesse.

In your pursuit to embody the lessons of the Femme Fatale Metamorphosis Effect, remember that true empowerment stems from within. Embrace your intelligence, hone your strategic acumen, and nurture your emotional intelligence. By embodying these qualities, you captivate others and inspire them to unlock their inner strength. Dare to be bold, dare to be brilliant – embrace the Femme Fatale Metamorphosis Effect within you and conquer the world with unwavering confidence.

3 Tips to Embracing the Essence of Feminine Allure

The allure of the Femme Fatale Metamorphosis Effect lies not only in her beauty but in her sensuality, a magnetic force that captivates all who encounter her. To truly embody this enchanting essence, one must delve deep into the realms of self-awareness and indulgence.

1. **Body Awareness**: Becomes the first step in this journey towards embracing sensuality. It is not merely about the physical form but how one moves and carries themselves through grace and poise. Every gesture and every step should exude a sense of confidence and allure, drawing others in with each movement.

2. **Dress the Part:** Follows suit, as the clothing we adorn ourselves with serves as an extension of our innermost desires and expressions. Choose garments that not only make you feel confident but also accentuate your best features. Let your style reflect your personality, a visual symphony that whispers secrets of your sensuality to the world.

3. **Sensory Indulgence:** Completes the trifecta, inviting you to engage your senses in experiences that bring pure pleasure. Whether it's savoring a delectable meal that ignites your taste buds, enveloping yourself in a favorite fragrance that lingers in the air like a whispered promise, or losing yourself in the melodies of music that stir your soul, each indulgence serves to heighten your sensual self.

In the dance of sensuality, we find the true essence of feminine allure. Embrace it, embody it, and let it weave its enchanting spell upon all who are fortunate enough to bask in your presence.

3 Tips Toward Embracing Your Inner Strength: The Power of Independence

In the journey of self-discovery and empowerment, independence stands as a cornerstone for every individual, especially for those with a fierce and captivating spirit. It is a quality that not only defines who we are but also shapes the path we tread on. So, how can one truly embody the essence of independence and unleash their inner Femme Fatale Metamorphosis Effect?

1.   **Self-Reliance:** To truly harness the power of independence, one must cultivate the art of self-reliance. It is about honing skills and building resources that enable you to stand tall on your own two feet. Financial independence holds the key to unlocking a realm of empowerment and freedom. By being self-sufficient, you pave the way for a life guided by your terms and choices.

2.   **Boundaries:** Setting and upholding healthy boundaries is a vital aspect of embracing independence. Knowing when to say no and safeguarding your time and energy from external influences is a mark of strength and self-respect. Boundaries serve as a shield, protecting your essence and ensuring that you navigate through life with grace and integrity.

3.   **Pursue Passions:** Your passions are the fuel that drives your spirit and ignites your soul. Engaging in activities and pursuits that resonate with your inner being is a profound way to cultivate independence. By immersing yourself in what brings you joy and fulfillment, you not only enrich your life but also amplify your sense of identity and self-worth. Your passions reflect your true essence and embracing them wholeheartedly is a testament to your fierce independence.

In the tapestry of life, independence weaves a thread of resilience, courage, and authenticity. It is a quality that sets you apart, allowing you to embrace your uniqueness and walk your path with confidence and grace. So, embrace your inner strength, honor your independence, and let your Femme Fatale Metamorphosis Effect spirit shine bright, illuminating the world with your unwavering presence.

4 Practical Exercises to Embody Your Femme Fatale Metamorphosis Effect

Are you ready to captivate the world with your irresistible allure and confidence?

Spend a few moments daily envisioning yourself as already being transformed by the Femme Fatale Metamorphosis Effect. Picture yourself exuding confidence, grace, and magnetism in every interaction. Visualize scenarios where you captivate others effortlessly with your charisma and allure.

1. Embrace the power of visualization techniques to embody the essence of a Femme Fatale Metamorphosis Effect like never before. Picture yourself as the epitome of charm, grace, and magnetism in every scenario you envision. Let your imagination run wild as you exude charisma and allure effortlessly.

2. Step into the realm of role-playing to finesse your social skills and persona. Engage in dynamic scenarios with a trusted confidant to perfect your introductions, negotiations, and flirtatious banter. Through these exercises, watch your self-assurance soar and your presence command attention in any setting.

3. Embrace the art of reflective journaling as you embark on your journey toward completing the ultimate Femme Fatale Metamorphosis Effect experience. Chronicle your

triumphs, setbacks, and personal growth as you navigate the path to self-discovery. Use your journal as a sanctuary to reinforce your ambitions and revel in your progress with each step forward.

4. Elevate your mindset with daily affirmations that solidify your Femme Fatale Metamorphosis Effect identity. Craft a repertoire of empowering statements that resonate with your inner strength and allure. Repeat phrases like "I am a force to be reckoned with," "I exude confidence and allure effortlessly," and "I embrace my sensuality as a source of power" to manifest your true potential.

Dare to unleash your inner Femme Fatale Metamorphosis Effect with these transformative strategies. Embrace your unique charm, confidence, and allure as you step into a world where you reign supreme. Let your journey toward self-discovery be a testament to your unwavering power and magnetism. Embrace the Femme Fatale Metamorphosis Effect within you and watch as the world becomes captivated by your irresistible persona.

3 Tips to Real-Life Applications of Femme Fatale Metamorphosis Effect Energy

In life, we are the weavers of our destiny, blending threads of strength, independence, and charisma to create a masterpiece that reflects our true essence. Let us delve into the realms of personal relationships, professional settings, and social situations, where our innate prowess shines brightest.

1. **Flourishing in Personal Relationships:** Within the intricate dance of love and connection, our Femme Fatale Metamorphosis Effect energy serves as a beacon, drawing partners who honor our independence and celebrate our

resilience. Embrace your inner allure, radiating a magnetic charm that captivates those who seek the intricacies of your spirit. Nurture the flames of passion by shrouding yourself in an enigmatic veil of mystery, unveiling new dimensions of your being to your beloved with each passing moment.

2. **Thriving in Professional Settings:** As we navigate the corridors of ambition and success, our confidence and strategic acumen pave the way for triumph in negotiations and leadership. Stand tall in the arena of professional discourse, exuding poise, and assertiveness as you carve a path toward your aspirations. Lead not with dominance, but with the wisdom of emotional intelligence, guiding others with a blend of authority and empathy that commands respect and admiration.

3. **Radiating in Social Situations:** In social interactions, our presence should be a symphony of grace and confidence, leaving an indelible mark on every soul we encounter. Become a beacon of connection in networking events, weaving meaningful conversations with threads of attentive listening and unwavering self-assurance. When the spotlight shines upon you, let your voice resonate with power, your body language speaks volumes, and your pauses echo with the weight of influence, captivating hearts, and minds with your undeniable charisma.

Embrace the essence of your being, for within you lies a reservoir of untapped potential waiting to be unleashed upon the world. Let your presence be a testament to the strength, independence, and allure that define you, illuminating every space you inhabit with the brilliance of your spirit. Embrace your power, and watch as the world unfolds before you, a canvas ripe for the strokes of your greatness.

Relationships thrive on a sense of intrigue and discovery. Rather than resorting to artificial mystery, cultivate a genuine sense of curiosity about yourself and your partner. Continuously explore new facets of your personality and share them openly, allowing the relationship to evolve and deepen organically.

By being true to yourself and remaining open to growth and vulnerability, you create a magnetic field that attracts genuine connections based on mutual understanding and respect. Embrace your authenticity, maintain a sense of wonder, and watch as your relationships flourish with depth, passion, and lasting fulfillment.

Final Thoughts on The Femme Fatale Metamorphosis Effect

In a world where confidence is key, mastering your Femme Fatale Metamorphosis Effect is a transformative journey towards embracing your inner strength and allure. It is not about becoming someone else but about unlocking the powerful aspects of who you already are.

To embark on this empowering path, start by cultivating self-confidence. Believe in your abilities and trust your instincts. Confidence radiates from within and captivates those around you, drawing them into your magnetic aura of self-assurance.

Maintain an air of mystery to keep others intrigued. Embrace the enigmatic qualities that make you unique and leave them wanting more. Mystery ignites curiosity and adds depth to your persona, making you even more captivating.

Harness your intelligence as a weapon of influence. Smart is the new sexy, and your intellect is a powerful tool in your arsenal. Use your wit and wisdom to navigate challenges and conquer obstacles with grace and finesse.

Embrace your sensuality with confidence and grace. Your allure lies in your ability to embrace your femininity and express your sensuality in a way that is authentic to you. Own your body and exude confidence in your skin, for true sensuality stems from self-acceptance and self-love.

Assert your independence and autonomy. A true Femme Fatale Metamorphosis Effect is a force to be reckoned with, standing strong in her beliefs and values. Embrace your independence and forge your path, unapologetically carving out your place in the world.

As you embrace your inner Femme Fatale Metamorphosis Effect experience, watch as your world transforms around you. You will radiate a magnetic charm and influence that captivates those around you, leaving a lasting impact wherever you go. Embrace your power, embrace your allure, and watch as you unleash the true essence of who you are - a woman of irresistible beauty, charm, and influence.

Chapter 3

The Evolution of Male Aesthetics Using Botulinum Neurotoxins, Dermal Fillers, and Permanent Makeup

Gone are the days when male grooming was considered a taboo subject. Today, a revolution is underway as men across the globe are embracing cosmetic procedures to redefine their appearance and exude confidence like never before. The era of Botulinum Neurotoxins, Dermal Fillers, and permanent makeup being solely reserved for women is a thing of the past, as more men than ever are stepping into the realm of aesthetic enhancements.

The shift in societal attitudes towards male grooming signifies a powerful movement towards self-expression and self-assurance. Men are no longer confined by traditional gender norms but are empowered to explore the limitless possibilities of cosmetic treatments to enhance their features and elevate their self-esteem. From smoothing out wrinkles with Botulinum Neurotoxins to sculpting a more defined jawline with Dermal Fillers, the options available to men today are as diverse as their individuality.

Embracing these cosmetic enhancements is not merely about changing one's physical appearance; it's about embracing one's true self and expressing it boldly to the world. The benefits of these treatments extend far beyond skin-deep transformations, delving into the realms of self-discovery and self-empowerment. By breaking free from societal constraints and embracing the power of male grooming, men can unlock a newfound sense of confidence and authenticity that radiates from within.

So, to all the men out there seeking to redefine their image and embrace their full potential, remember this: cosmetic enhancements are not just about looking good, but about feeling great. It's about stepping into a new era of self-expression and confidence, where the only limit is your imagination. Embrace the power of male grooming, unleash your true self, and let your confidence shine brighter than ever before.

Masculinity Redefined: The Evolution of Male Aesthetics

The evolving landscape of societal norms has ushered in a new era where masculinity intertwines seamlessly with self-care. Today, men are embracing a diverse array of grooming practices, transcending traditional boundaries, and delving into cosmetic procedures once deemed exclusive to women.

The modern man is no longer bound by outdated stereotypes but instead revels in the freedom to express himself through grooming choices that align with his personal style and preferences. From facials to hair removal and beyond, the realm of male grooming has expanded exponentially, offering a plethora of options to enhance one's appearance and self-confidence.

Embracing this cultural shift signifies a departure from the conventional narrative of masculinity, paving the way for a more inclusive and accepting society. By shattering preconceived notions of what it means to be a man, individuals are empowered to explore and embrace their unique sense of self, unencumbered by societal expectations.

In this new era of male grooming, beauty knows no bounds, and self-care transcends gender norms. It is a celebration of individuality, a testament to the evolving perceptions of masculinity, and a reflection of the progressive mindset that defines the modern man. So, let us embrace this newfound freedom, unlock our grooming potential, and redefine what it means to look and feel our best, inside and out.

Factors Driving the Shift

- **Changing Beauty Standards:** With the rise of social media and celebrity influence, there is increased pressure on men to maintain a youthful and attractive appearance.

- **Professional Advancement:** In competitive industries where image matters, maintaining a polished and youthful look can give men a competitive edge.

- **Self-Confidence:** Cosmetic procedures can help men feel more confident and comfortable in their own skin, leading to improved self-esteem and overall well-being.

Revitalizing Men's Aesthetics: The Power of Botulinum Neurotoxins

Botulinum Neurotoxins, popularly recognized under brand names like Botox, Daxxify, Dysport, and Xeomin, are potent proteins utilized to temporarily diminish the visibility of wrinkles and fine lines by easing facial muscles. Despite being traditionally linked with women, the benefits of Botulinum Neurotoxins extend to men as well, offering a gateway to a revitalized appearance.

· *Smoothing Forehead Lines:* Men often find themselves with distinctive horizontal lines etched on their foreheads, a result of repetitive facial gestures. Botulinum Neurotoxins prove effective in ironing out these lines, bestowing a rejuvenated and youthful semblance.

· *Softening Crow's Feet:* The presence of wrinkles encircling the eyes, commonly referred to as crow's feet, can project an older and fatigued look. Botulinum Neurotoxins step in to diminish these lines, injecting a touch of vitality and vigor into one's countenance.

·   ***Addressing Frown Lines:*** Profound lines nestled between the eyebrows, colloquially known as frown lines or "11" lines, can inadvertently lend a harsh or stern air to a man's face. Botulinum Neurotoxins offer a remedy by gently smoothing these lines, cultivating a warmer and more approachable visage.

·   ***Gummy Smile Reduction:*** By limiting the movement of the upper lip muscles, Botox can prevent excessive gum exposure when smiling. This results in a more balanced and aesthetically pleasing smile, with less gum tissue visible.

In essence, Botulinum Neurotoxins present men with a pathway to reclaiming their youthful masculinity and revitalizing their overall appearance. Embrace the transformative power of these neurotoxic proteins to redefine your aesthetic journey and unlock a newfound sense of confidence and allure.

Discover the Benefits of Dermal Fillers for Men

Dermal Fillers, typically associated with women, are versatile injectable gels that offer a range of advantages for men as well. These fillers are designed to add volume, refine contours, and minimize the appearance of wrinkles and folds. Here are some key benefits that Dermal Fillers can provide specifically for men:

·   **Restoring Facial Volume:** Men, like women, may experience volume loss in areas such as the cheeks, resulting in a sunken or hollow look. By replenishing lost volume, Dermal Fillers can help create a more youthful and masculine facial contour.

·   **Enhancing Jawline and Chin Definition:** A strong and well-defined jawline is a coveted masculine feature.

Dermal Fillers combined with Botulinum Neurotoxins can be strategically applied to enhance jawline contours and chin, giving men a more sculpted and rejuvenated look.

· **Add Volume to Lips:** Men, much like women struggle with the visual appearance of thin or asymmetrical lips. Dermal Fillers alone or combined with Botulinum Neurotoxins can create a more balanced and fuller look and feel to the appearance and touch of the lips.

In conclusion, Dermal Fillers are not just for women – they are a valuable tool for men seeking to rejuvenate their appearance and enhance their facial features. With the ability to restore volume, soften lines, and define contours, Dermal Fillers offer a subtle yet effective way for men to achieve a more youthful and refined look."

Enhancing Features with Micropigmentation and Microblading for Men

In recent years, the trend of permanent makeup has transcended traditional gender norms, with an increasing number of men opting for techniques like eyebrow microblading, scalp, and facial micropigmentation to enhance their features by filling in areas with replicated hair strokes. The benefits of permanent makeup for men are multifaceted and go beyond mere aesthetics:

· **Addressing Sparse Areas of Hair**: Genetics, folliculitis, and thinning hair can result in uneven or sparse scalp and facial hair for some men. Micropigmentation also known as Permanent Makeup or Cosmetic Tattooing offers a solution by filling in these areas with simulated hair strokes that mimic the look of hair strands and hair follicles, creating a fuller appearance of hair that can significantly enhance one's overall look.

· **Defining Brow Shape:** Well-defined eyebrows play a crucial role in framing the face and enhancing facial symmetry. Through Permanent Makeup, men can achieve a more defined and polished eyebrow shape that complements their unique features, giving them a more refined and put-together appearance.

By embracing the possibilities offered by permanent eyebrow makeup, men can achieve subtle yet impactful enhancements that not only redefine their facial aesthetics but also empower them to present their best selves to the world. The growing popularity of these techniques underscores the shifting attitudes towards male grooming and the increasing importance placed on self-care and personal presentation in today's society.

Unveiling the Modern Man: Overcoming Stigma and Stereotypes

In a world where self-care and grooming have become increasingly prevalent, the topic of male aesthetics has sparked discussions around stigma and stereotypes that may still linger. While societal norms continue to evolve, there remains a need to confront and dismantle any lingering misconceptions surrounding men's engagement with cosmetic procedures.

Embracing cosmetic procedures is a bold declaration of self-love and empowerment. By advocating for inclusivity and fostering an environment of acceptance, we pave the way for a future where beauty knows no gender boundaries. The narrative of masculinity has long been intertwined with notions of ruggedness and stoicism, often overshadowing the idea of men embracing beauty rituals or enhancements. Despite progress in breaking down these barriers, it is crucial to address any lingering stigma that may hinder individuals from exploring their aesthetic preferences freely.

By challenging these outdated perceptions, we pave the way for a more inclusive and accepting society that celebrates diversity in beauty practices. Empowering individuals, regardless of gender, to make choices that align with their personal goals and desires is a step toward creating a culture that values self-expression and authenticity.

As we redefine traditional beauty standards and embrace a more holistic view of grooming and aesthetics, it is essential to recognize and celebrate the uniqueness of each individual journey toward self-improvement and self-expression. Let us continue to champion inclusivity and empowerment, fostering a world where beauty knows no bounds and where everyone can feel confident in their own skin.

Promoting Gender-Neutral Beauty

In a contemporary landscape where standards of beauty continue to evolve, the notion of gender-neutral beauty has emerged as a potent agent of change. By championing inclusivity and honoring individual preferences, we have the opportunity to lay the foundation for a more varied and welcoming society.

Education plays a pivotal role in the reshaping of societal perspectives. By illuminating the positive impacts that cosmetic procedures can have on individuals of all genders, we can challenge preconceived notions and cultivate a climate of empathy. Furthermore, by presenting a broad spectrum of representations in both media and advertising, we can assist in normalizing diverse manifestations of beauty.

Central to the concept of gender-neutral beauty is the principle of empowerment. Every individual should be afforded the liberty to make choices regarding their appearance without apprehension of censure or social stigma. By advocating for open discourse and acceptance, we can establish an environment where personal decisions are revered and upheld.

In Respect of Personal Choice in Beauty

In the current dynamic societal landscape, the pursuit of self-discovery and empowerment is boundless. All individuals, including men, are entitled to experience confidence and ease in their own identity. Cosmetic procedures, once stigmatized for men, now serve as a means of self-expression and empowerment.

A wide array of options, ranging from Botulinum Neurotoxins to Dermal Fillers and Permanent Makeup, cater to individuals seeking to refine their appearance and elevate their self-assurance. By transcending archaic gender norms and stereotypes, men are unlocking opportunities for personal expression and growth.

In a society that promotes inclusivity and celebrates diversity, the beauty industry plays a crucial role. It has the capacity to cultivate an environment where individuals of all genders can confidently and proudly manifest their true selves. This movement is not solely about external transformations but also about embracing our authentic selves holistically.

Let us embark on a journey of self-discovery and self-acceptance, where each decision reflects our distinct identity and personal evolution. Let us honor the richness of diversity and individuality, recognizing that genuine confidence emanates from embracing our true selves. It is time to reshape the discourse, catalyzing progress through each cosmetic enhancement and paving the way for a future where everyone is empowered to radiate their unique brilliance.

Chapter 4

Decoding the Perfect Timing to Explore Non-Invasive Cosmetic Treatments

Embracing Your Beauty Journey: A Timeless Exploration

In a world where self-care and enhancement options are plentiful, the decision of when to embark on a beauty transformation journey is a deeply personal one. From the allure of Botulinum Neurotoxins to the artistry of Dermal Fillers and the convenience of Permanent Makeup, the realm of cosmetic procedures beckons with promises of rejuvenation and enhancement.

But beyond the allure of immediate results lies a crucial consideration - timing. When is the right age to delve into these transformative treatments? The answer, it seems, is as diverse as the individuals contemplating them. Each person's path to self-discovery, self-care, and self-expression is unique and guided by personal preferences, values, and aspirations.

As we navigate the vast landscape of beauty enhancements, it becomes apparent that age is but a number in the grand scheme of self-improvement. The true key lies in understanding oneself, embracing one's journey, and honoring the process of self-evolution. Whether it's a subtle enhancement or a bold transformation, the decision to explore cosmetic procedures should be rooted in self-love, respect, and a deep commitment to one's well-being.

So, let us embark on this beauty journey with a sense of wonder and empowerment, knowing that the canvas of our bodies is a reflection of our inner spirit. Let us embrace the beauty of transformation at every age, honoring the wisdom that comes with experience and the courage to redefine ourselves on our terms.

In the palette of life, each choice we make adds a brushstroke to the portrait of who we are becoming. Let us paint our enchanting story with intention, grace, and an unwavering belief in our inherent worth. For true beauty knows no bounds, transcending age and time to illuminate the essence of our being.

The Science of Aging and Cosmetic Procedures

To truly grasp the significance of age-appropriate cosmetic procedures, it's crucial to first familiarize ourselves with the intricate mechanisms of the aging process and its impact on the skin and facial features. Aging, a complex interplay of intrinsic and extrinsic factors, encompasses a myriad of influences such as genetic predispositions, sun exposure, lifestyle preferences, and hormonal fluctuations. Manifestations of aging typically include:

· **Fine lines and wrinkles:** These imperfections arise from the natural decline in collagen and elastin synthesis, leading to diminished skin firmness and elasticity.

· **Volume loss:** Depletion of facial fat and bone density over time can result in a loss of facial fullness, contributing to hollowed cheeks and sunken temples.

· **Skin Laxity:** The gradual decline in skin elasticity can cause the skin to lose its tautness, resulting in sagging and drooping in various facial areas.

· **Uneven Pigmentation:** Factors like sun exposure and hormonal imbalances can trigger irregular pigmentation concerns, such as hyperpigmentation and age spots.

· **Thinning and Balding Hair:** Typically, with aging, hair growth patterns decelerate, and hair follicles may tend to diminish in size, causing strands of hair to appear thinner.

Understanding these fundamental aspects of aging provides a solid foundation for exploring the nuances of age-appropriate cosmetic interventions.

3 Factors to Keep in Mind Before Opting for Cosmetic Procedures

Deciding on the optimal age for undergoing cosmetic procedures involves a multifaceted evaluation process. Here are some key considerations to ponder:

1. Unique Aging Patterns

· **Genetic Influence:** The pace and visibility of aging are substantially impacted by genetics. Certain individuals might experience premature wrinkles and loss of volume compared to others.

· **Lifestyle Factors:** Factors like sun exposure, smoking, dietary choices, and skincare routines can either hasten or decelerate the aging trajectory. Those with sun-damaged skin or unhealthy lifestyle practices might contemplate treatments at an earlier stage.

2. Objectives and Anticipations of Treatment

· Proactive Versus Reactive Approaches: While some individuals prefer early interventions as a preventive strategy to impede aging, others seek treatments primarily to address existing signs of aging.

· Realistic Outlook: Managing expectations regarding the potential outcomes of cosmetic procedures is paramount. Grasping the limitations and possibilities of each treatment aids in establishing feasible goals.

3. Consultation with a Competent Practitioner

· **Personalized Assessment:** Engaging in a consultation with a seasoned and qualified practitioner is pivotal for evaluating the individual's skin condition, concerns, and aspirations.

· **Tailored Treatment Regimen:** Post-assessment, the practitioner can devise a customized treatment plan that addresses the individual's specific requirements and age-related transformations.

By taking into account these factors and engaging in thorough deliberation, individuals can make informed decisions regarding the appropriate timing for embarking on cosmetic enhancements.

Botulinum Neurotoxins: A Guide to Age-Appropriate Use

Suggested Age: Botulinum neurotoxins, including popular brands like Botox, Daxxify, Dysport, and Xeomin, have become go-to treatments for combatting dynamic wrinkles caused by repetitive muscle movements. Deciding on the right age to consider these treatments involves a mix of personal factors and cosmetic goals.

·   **Early 20s to 30s:** Some individuals may opt for Botulinum Neurotoxins as a proactive measure to prevent wrinkle formation. This age group might choose to start treatments in their mid-20s, while others may wait until their 30s when fine lines start to appear more prominently.

·   **Late 30s and 40s:** Many people begin noticing more visible wrinkles that may prompt them to seek Botulinum Neurotoxin injections. These treatments can help soften lines and preserve a youthful look as signs of aging become more noticeable.

·   **50s and beyond**: Botulinum Neurotoxins can still be effective in addressing dynamic wrinkles, especially around the eyes, forehead, and mouth. Individuals in this age group can benefit from treatments to rejuvenate their appearance and maintain skin vitality.

Ultimately, the decision to use Botulinum Neurotoxins should be based on individual preferences, skin conditions, and desired outcomes. Consulting with a qualified aesthetic cosmetic injector can help determine the best approach for achieving a refreshed and youthful look at any age.

Dermal Fillers: A Guide to Age-Appropriate Use

Suggested Age: Dermal Fillers offer a versatile solution to restore volume, refine contours, and reduce the appearance of wrinkles and folds, providing a rejuvenated and youthful look. The appropriate age to consider Dermal Fillers is a personal decision that depends on individual aging patterns and cosmetic goals. Let's explore the optimal age ranges for utilizing Dermal Fillers:

·   **Early 20s to 30s:** Early signs of aging, such as volume loss and fine lines, may prompt some individuals to consider Dermal Fillers in their mid to late 20s. These injections can help enhance facial contours and address subtle changes in the skin.

·   **Late 30s and 40s:** As individuals reach their 30s to 40s, noticeable volume loss becomes more prevalent, especially in areas like the cheeks, temples, and lips. Dermal Fillers are highly effective in replenishing lost volume and revitalizing the facial appearance during this stage of life.

·   **50s and beyond**: For individuals aged 50 and beyond, Dermal Fillers continue to offer significant benefits by targeting deeper wrinkles, sagging skin, and hollowed areas that naturally occur with age. These fillers can provide a more youthful and refreshed look, enhancing overall facial aesthetics.

Ultimately, the decision to undergo Dermal Filler treatment should be based on individual needs and desired outcomes. Consulting with a qualified aesthetic cosmetic injector is essential to determine the most suitable approach for achieving your cosmetic objectives. Embrace the opportunity to enhance your natural beauty and restore a more youthful appearance with the transformative effects of Dermal Fillers.

Permanent Makeup: A Guide to Age-Appropriate Use

Suggested Age: Permanent Makeup, a revolutionary cosmetic procedure encompassing techniques like microblading, eyeliner, lip blushing, cheek blushing and more offers a transformative enhancement of one's facial features that transcends age boundaries. The decision to embrace Permanent Makeup is a deeply personal one, influenced by individual tastes and lifestyle choices.

In the realm of age considerations, the landscape of Permanent Makeup application is as diverse as the individuals who seek its allure:

Early 20s to 30s: For some, the allure of Permanent Makeup beckons in the tender years of late adolescence or the dawn of early adulthood. This age group may opt for Permanent Makeup procedures to subtly enhance their natural features, correct imperfections, or simply experiment with newfound expressions of self.

Late 30s and 40s: The realm of Permanent Makeup extends a welcoming hand to individuals in their 30s and beyond, offering a sanctuary where the pursuit of a refined and polished appearance seamlessly intertwines with the desire for convenience. For those seeking to maintain a sophisticated allure without the rigors of daily makeup application, Permanent Makeup emerges as a trusted confidant.

50s and beyond: For individuals in their 50s and beyond, Permanent Makeup can be a transformative tool in enhancing features while embracing the natural aging process. It serves as a way to accentuate key facial elements and boost confidence without the need for constant touch-ups.

The right age for embracing Permanent Makeup supersedes the confines of numerical digits, it's a narrative that celebrates individuality, self-expression, and the effortless pursuit of satisfaction. Whether you are a blossoming ingenue, a seasoned sophisticate, or a cosmopolitan trendsetter, the allure of Permanent Makeup beckons, promising a natural or elaborate channel suitable for both men and women.

Final Thoughts on Age-Appropriate Uses

Embarking on the journey towards rejuvenation and enhancement through cosmetic procedures is a personal and transformative experience. The decision to undergo treatments such as Botulinum Neurotoxins, Dermal Fillers, and Permanent Makeup is influenced by a multitude of factors, making the timing of these interventions a crucial consideration.

Age, a key determinant in the realm of cosmetic enhancements, plays a significant role in the decision-making process. However, there is no one-size-fits-all answer to the question of when is the ideal age to pursue these treatments. The right timing varies from person to person, contingent upon individual aging patterns, treatment objectives, and lifestyle choices.

Chapter 5

The Benefits of Exclusivity in the Privileged Realm of Concierge Beauty Services

In the modern era, where time is of the essence, the demand for convenience and tailored services has reached new heights. One emerging trend that exemplifies this shift is the rise of beauty concierge services. These services cater to individuals seeking aesthetic treatments such as Botulinum Neurotoxins and Dermal Fillers, all in the comfort of their own homes or preferred locations.

The appeal of beauty concierge services lies in their ability to provide personalized care and attention to clients who value efficiency and flexibility in their busy schedules. By offering on-site treatments, these services eliminate the need for clients to travel to a salon or clinic, saving them valuable time and effort.

Clients from various walks of life benefit from beauty concierge services. Busy professionals, stay-at-home parents, and individuals with mobility issues are just a few examples of those who find these services invaluable. For many, the convenience of receiving aesthetic treatments at home allows them to integrate self-care into their hectic routines seamlessly.

The decision to opt for beauty concierge services is often motivated by a desire for a more personalized and convenient experience. By choosing to incorporate these bespoke services into their lives, clients can enjoy the benefits of professional aesthetic treatments without sacrificing their precious time.

Beauty concierge services represent a modern solution for individuals seeking high-quality aesthetic treatments tailored to their specific needs. By bringing the med spa experience to the client's doorstep, these services offer a unique and convenient approach to self-care in today's fast-paced world.

The Beauty Concierge Experience

Step into a realm where beauty transcends mere aesthetics and becomes a transformative journey of self-care and empowerment. Imagine a sanctuary where luxury meets convenience, where the essence of beauty is not confined within the walls of a clinic but delivered right to your doorstep. This is the promise of beauty concierge services – a revolution in the realm of self-care.

Gone are the days of cumbersome appointments and crowded waiting rooms. Embrace a new era where your well-being takes center stage, where personalized attention is not just a luxury but a fundamental principle. With beauty concierge services available, the world of beauty is redefined as a deeply personal experience tailored to your preferred location.

Picture this: a serene oasis in the midst of your bustling life, where skilled professionals curate treatments specifically designed to enhance your natural beauty. Whether in the comfort of your home, the privacy of your office, or the extravagance of a special event, beauty concierge services bring the spa to you, ensuring that self-care seamlessly integrates into your lifestyle.

What sets these services apart are the key features that prioritize your comfort and satisfaction

·   **Convenience:** Say goodbye to the stress of scheduling appointments during your busy day. With beauty concierge services, treatments are tailored to your schedule and location, ensuring that your beauty routine fits seamlessly into your lifestyle.

·   **Privacy:** Enjoy the luxury of discretion with beauty treatments in the comfort of your own space. No more awkward encounters or public waiting rooms — just a personalized experience focused entirely on your well-being.

·   **Personalized Attention:** Experience the undivided care and attention of a skilled practitioner who is dedicated to understanding your unique needs. Say hello to a customized approach to beauty and wellness that is tailored exclusively for you.

It's not just about pampering; it's about self-love. Each treatment is a celebration of your individuality, a reflection of your inner radiance brought to the surface. Beauty concierge services empower you to embrace your true self, to nurture your body and soul in a way that resonates with your essence.

So, say goodbye to the ordinary and welcome the extraordinary. Embrace the future of beauty services with open arms, where convenience, privacy, and personalized attention converge to elevate your beauty experience to new heights. Let beauty concierge services be your guide on a journey of self-discovery and self-care, where beauty is not just a reflection in the mirror but a radiant glow that emanates from within.

Who Benefits from Beauty Concierge Services

1. Celebrities and High-Profile Individuals

If you're tired of sacrificing your privacy and precious time for Cosmetic Injection Dermal Filler and Botulinum

Neurotoxin services, look no further than exclusive concierge services tailored for high-profile individuals like you.

Say goodbye to paparazzi and public scrutiny by indulging in discreet treatments delivered right to your doorstep. Beauty concierge services offer several advantages for these clients:

- **Discreet Treatments:** Privacy is non-negotiable when it comes to celebrities, and our concierge skincare services understand the importance of keeping your beauty regimen under wraps. Enjoy the luxury of pampering yourself in the comfort of your own home or any private location of your choice, away from prying eyes.
- **Flexible Scheduling:** Forget about the hassle of fitting clinic visits into your busy filming, event, or travel schedules. Concierge services are designed to cater to your every need, offering flexible scheduling that aligns perfectly with your timetable.
- **Tailored Care:** We understand that consistent results are paramount for high-profile individuals, and our expert team is dedicated to ensuring that you receive the tailored care you deserve. From customized treatments to exclusive products.

2. Busy Professionals

In today's fast-paced world, busy professionals are constantly juggling demanding careers, leaving little time for self-care. However, a revolutionary solution has emerged in the form of beauty concierge services, offering a unique approach to maintaining beauty routines amidst hectic schedules.

·   **Streamlined Time Management:** One of the key benefits of beauty concierge services is the time efficiency they offer. By eliminating the need to travel to a clinic, professionals can save valuable time that would have otherwise been spent commuting. Whether it's scheduling treatments during lunch breaks, after work hours, or even while on business trips, these services provide the flexibility that modern professionals need to stay on top of their beauty regimen.

·   **Convenient On-Site Services**: For individuals constantly on the move, the convenience of having a beauty practitioner come directly to their office or hotel is unparalleled. This on-site service not only saves time but also eliminates the hassle of navigating through traffic or finding a suitable location for beauty treatments. By bringing the expertise directly to the client, beauty concierge services cater to the needs of busy professionals in a way that fits seamlessly into their hectic lifestyles.

·   **Stress-Free Beauty Maintenance:** The ability to receive beauty treatments in a familiar and comfortable environment can significantly reduce stress levels for busy professionals. By transforming everyday spaces like offices or hotel rooms into personalized beauty sanctuaries, these services create a calming oasis amidst the chaos of work life. This stress-free approach to beauty maintenance ensures that professionals can prioritize self-care without adding unnecessary pressure to their already busy schedules.

3. Clients with Special Needs or Mobility Issues

Catering to clients with special needs or mobility challenges is a crucial aspect of providing holistic care. Beauty concierge services have emerged as a beacon of accessibility and comfort for individuals facing these unique circumstances.

· **Accessibility Beyond Boundaries:** The beauty concierge model breaks down barriers by offering services that transcend traditional clinic settings. For those with mobility issues, the ability to receive top-notch beauty treatments without the hassle of traveling is truly liberating. Whether it's a facial, massage, or skincare regimen, practitioners bring their expertise directly to the client's doorstep.

· **Comfort in Familiarity:** Stepping into a clinic can be daunting for many, especially for those with health concerns or disabilities. By opting for beauty concierge services, clients can revel in the comfort of their own space. Familiar surroundings can foster a sense of relaxation, contributing to a positive overall experience.

· **Tailored Care, Enhanced Safety:** Every individual is unique, and so are their needs. Beauty concierge services excel in providing tailored care that prioritizes the client's well-being. By customizing treatments to suit specific requirements, practitioners ensure that safety is never compromised. This personalized approach instills confidence and trust, fostering long-lasting relationships built on care and understanding.

4. Anyone Valuing Time and Convenience

In our fast-paced world, time is a precious commodity that many individuals hold in high regard, regardless of their occupation or social standing. The quest for convenience permeates every aspect of modern life, prompting the emergence of beauty concierge services to meet the needs of a diverse clientele. These specialized services offer a range of benefits tailored to the time-conscious consumer:

·   **Tailored Scheduling:** Beauty concierge services prioritize flexibility by accommodating appointments at times that align with the client's daily schedule, be it early mornings, late evenings, or weekends. This personalized approach ensures that clients can enjoy treatments without disrupting their routines.

·   **Home Comfort:** One of the key advantages of beauty concierge services is the ability to receive treatments in the comfort of one's own home. By eliminating the need to travel to a med spa, clients can relax in familiar surroundings, enhancing the overall experience and promoting a sense of tranquility.

·   **Personalized Care:** Building a consistent relationship with a beauty concierge practitioner allows clients to receive personalized care that caters to their individual needs and preferences. By understanding the client's unique requirements, practitioners can deliver tailored treatments that yield optimal results and foster a deeper sense of trust and satisfaction.

Final Thoughts on the Luxury Beauty Concierge Service

Beauty concierge services have emerged as the pinnacle of customized and convenient beauty care, serving a wide spectrum of clientele ranging from celebrities to individuals with hectic schedules. These services redefine the traditional approach to aesthetic treatments by delivering top-tier services directly to the client, thereby eradicating the challenges and pressures associated with conventional med spa visits. The essence of beauty concierge services lies in providing an elite and individualized experience that caters to the unique needs and preferences of each client.

The allure of beauty concierge services transcends mere convenience; it embodies a paradigm shift in how individuals pursue and uphold their beauty aspirations. Whether seeking utmost privacy, unparalleled convenience, or specialized care, beauty concierge services offer a transformative experience that elevates the beauty journey to new heights. By combining luxury with personalized attention, these services empower clients to achieve their beauty goals in a manner that is both seamless and indulgent.

In a fast-paced world where time is of the essence, beauty concierge services stand out as a beacon of efficiency and sophistication. By bridging the gap between premium beauty treatments and the demands of modern life, these services pave the way for a holistic approach to beauty that is centered around the client's individuality and comfort. Embracing the ethos of exclusivity and excellence, beauty concierge services are redefining the beauty industry landscape by offering a bespoke and unparalleled beauty experience.

In essence, beauty concierge services herald a new era of personalized beauty services that prioritize the client's needs above all else. Through a fusion of luxury, convenience, and customization, these services not only meet but exceed the expectations of today's discerning clientele. By embracing the philosophy of tailor-made beauty solutions, beauty concierge services are reshaping the way individuals engage with beauty, setting a new standard of care and sophistication in the process.

Chapter 6

Elevate Your Social Gathering by Hosting a Cosmetic Injection Party with Botulinum Neurotoxins and Dermal Fillers

Indulge in a luxurious and personalized beauty experience with concierge services that prioritize your well-being and satisfaction. From customized scheduling to on-site pampering, these services are designed to make you feel pampered and valued every step of the way. Experience the ultimate in luxury self-care with beauty concierge services – because you deserve nothing but the best.

What to Expect

1. Tailored Virtual Consultation Experience a personalized assessment where your goals, medical history, and treatment options are thoroughly discussed to craft a customized plan that suits your individual needs and lifestyle.

2. Seamless Treatment Day Enjoy a professional setup with all necessary equipment brought to your chosen location, creating a relaxed and private environment for you to receive top-notch care. Benefit from personal attention and immediate feedback for optimal results.

3. Continued Support and Care Receive detailed aftercare instructions post-treatment, and rest assured knowing that your practitioner is always available to address any queries or concerns. Nurture an ongoing relationship that fosters trust and ensures consistent care for long-term beauty goals.

Revolutionize Your Beauty Experience with Glamour Injections Parties

Experience the Glamour of a Cosmetic Injection Party

Elevate your social gathering to a whole new level of luxury and sophistication. Say goodbye to mundane meetups and hello to the ultimate fusion of beauty and bonding with our exclusive Glamour Gatherings with a qualified cosmetic injector

Unleash the power of transformation as you and your friends immerse yourselves in a world of beauty with our Glamour Gatherings. Picture this: a chic and stylish setting, where a skilled practitioner works their magic with Botulinum Neurotoxins and Dermal Fillers, enhancing your natural beauty in a social and vibrant atmosphere.

Educate and Elevate

Knowledge is power, especially when it comes to your beauty regimen. Glamour Gatherings go beyond aesthetics, offering an educational experience where you can learn about the latest treatments, techniques, and trends in a relaxed and informative setting. Ask questions, get insights, and embark on a journey to enhance your beauty knowledge.

Unveil Exclusive Offers

Prepare to be dazzled with special discounts and incentives exclusively available at Glamour Gatherings.

The Glamour Gathering Advantage

1. **Elevated Bonding:** Forge deeper connections with your friends as you share laughter, stories, and unforgettable moments at our Glamour Gatherings. It's not just about beauty; it's about building lasting memories in a supportive and uplifting environment.

2. **Celebrate in Style:** Immerse yourself in a celebratory ambiance filled with music, refreshments, and a touch of glamour. Let the festive vibes elevate your spirits as you indulge in a pampering experience like no other.

3. **Convenience Redefined:** Simplify your beauty routine by hosting a Glamour Gathering where you can enjoy multiple treatments in one convenient location. Embrace the comfort of receiving cosmetic enhancements in a familiar and welcoming setting surrounded by friends.

4. **Empower Your Beauty Journey:** Receive expert guidance from qualified practitioners who are dedicated to helping you achieve your beauty goals. Participate in engaging Q&A sessions to gain insights into the world of cosmetic enhancements and make informed decisions about your beauty regimen.

Elevate Your Beauty Experience with Glamour Gatherings

Embarking on the path of aesthetic enhancement is a thrilling adventure that requires careful consideration and discernment. The key to achieving stunning results lies in the selection of a reputable beauty concierge cosmetic injector who will guide you through the road to Botulinum Neurotoxins and Dermal Fillers.

Chapter 7

Selecting Your Perfect Practitioner: Choosing the Right Match

Finding the perfect practitioner is akin to discovering a trusted confidant who unlocks your inner radiance. Your journey towards enhancing your beauty should be guided by skilled hands that exude expertise and artistry.

Key Elements to Consider When Selecting Your Aesthetic Partner

When it comes to enhancing your beauty, the significance of choosing a competent and experienced practitioner cannot be overstated. Here's why:

·   **Safety:** Entrusting your aesthetic treatments to a qualified practitioner significantly reduces the likelihood of complications and adverse effects. Your well-being is paramount, and a skilled professional will prioritize your safety throughout the process.

·   **Effectiveness:** A seasoned expert possesses the finesse and expertise needed to deliver results that are not only aesthetically pleasing but also enhance your natural features. Achieving a harmonious and balanced look requires precision and artistry, qualities that a proficient practitioner can offer.

Confidence: Knowing you are in capable hands allows you to proceed with confidence and peace of mind.

Qualifications and Certifications

1. Botulinum Neurotoxins Practitioners

Botulinum Neurotoxins treatments require precise injections into specific muscles to achieve the desired effect without compromising facial expression.

- **Operations Facility/ Concierge:** Ensure your Cosmetic Injector is partnered with a Medical Director on record as per Texas state law to legally perform Botulinum Neurotoxin injection services via practitioner's facility and/ or concierge beauty service visit. Additional cosmetic injector practitioner laws and mandates vary per state.

- **Medical/ Cosmetic Aesthetics Background:** Look for practitioners who are licensed and certified medical aesthetics professionals.

- **Certification and Training:** Look for additional certification in Botulinum Neurotoxins techniques from recognized institutions.

- **Experience:** Ask about their experience with Botulinum Neurotoxins. How many procedures have they performed? Do they stay updated with the latest techniques and safety protocols?

- **Portfolio:** A reputable practitioner should have a portfolio of before-and-after photos showcasing their work. This gives you an idea of their aesthetic style and expertise.

2. Dermal Fillers Practitioners

Dermal Fillers involve injecting substances to add volume, enhance contours, and smooth lines. Precision and artistry are key.

- **Operations Facility/ Concierge:** Ensure your Cosmetic Injector is partnered with a Medical Director on record as per Texas state law to legally perform Dermal Filler injection services via practitioner's facility and/ or concierge beauty service visit. Additional cosmetic injector practitioner laws and mandates vary per state.

- **Medical/ Cosmetic Aesthetics Background:** Similar to Dermal Filler, choose practitioners who are licensed and certified medical aesthetics professionals.

- **Certification and Training:** Look for additional certification in Dermal Filler techniques from recognized institutions.

- **Experience:** Ask about their experience with Dermal Fillers. How many procedures have they performed? Do they stay updated with the latest techniques and safety protocols?

- **Portfolio:** A reputable practitioner should have a portfolio of before-and-after photos showcasing their work. This gives you an idea of their aesthetic style and expertise.

3. Permanent Makeup Practitioners

Permanent Makeup requires a different skill set, focusing on artistry and knowledge of skin behavior.

- **Operations Facility:** Ensure your practitioner is providing services based in a licensed facility (tattoo studio) to ensure compliance with local zoning laws and mandates.

- **Background in Skincare:** Although Permanent Makeup results are mostly based on the practitioner's technique and artistry, a background in skincare is imperative to ensuring your client does not have a condition of the skin that may be considered a contraindication.

- **Certification and Training:** Ensure the practitioner is formally trained in Permanent Makeup, micropigmentation, or cosmetic tattooing, adhering to local regulations and zoning requirements.

- **Artistic Skill:** Since Permanent Makeup is akin to tattooing, the practitioner should have a keen eye for detail and a good sense of aesthetics.

- **Portfolio:** A reputable practitioner should have a portfolio of before-and-after photos showcasing their work. This gives you an idea of their aesthetic style and expertise.

The quest for the perfect cosmetic practitioner begins with a focus on qualifications. Ensuring that the professional you select is highly trained, certified, and experienced in the specific procedures you are seeking is paramount. By prioritizing qualifications, you lay a solid foundation for a successful aesthetic journey.

Engaging in detailed consultations is another key step on the path to finding the right cosmetic practitioner. Take the time to meet with different professionals, ask questions, and express your aesthetic goals and concerns. A good practitioner will listen attentively, address your queries, and offer personalized recommendations tailored to your unique needs.

Above all, remember that the pursuit of aesthetic enhancement is not just about the end results—it is also about the journey itself. By investing time and effort into selecting a practitioner who prioritizes your safety, satisfaction, and well-being, you are laying the groundwork for a rewarding experience that goes beyond physical transformation.

The road to achieving your aesthetic aspirations is paved with careful choices and informed decisions. By selecting a cosmetic practitioner who meets your criteria for expertise, conducting thorough research, and engaging in detailed consultations, you are setting yourself up for success. Trust your instincts, prioritize your well-being, and embrace the journey with confidence and peace of mind. Your cosmetic aesthetic goals await, and with the right practitioner by your side, the possibilities are endless.

Final Thoughts on Selecting Your Perfect Practitioner

Selecting the perfect practitioner for your aesthetic metamorphosis is a weighty decision requiring meticulous consideration. By placing qualifications at the forefront, embarking on thorough research endeavors, and engaging in exhaustive consultations, you're on the path to not only enhancing your appearance but also ensuring your safety and contentment.

Your aesthetic odyssey should be as fulfilling as the results it yields. Invest time in making informed decisions and watch as your aesthetic aspirations materialize with confidence and tranquility. Let your journey to aesthetic magnificence be a testament to the transformative power of informed choices.

Chapter 8

The Virtual Aesthetic Experience: Modernizing Consultations for Ease and Efficiency

In this era of digital transformation, the realm of aesthetic enhancements has embraced a new frontier with the rise of virtual consultations. No longer confined to in-person visits at med spas, individuals can now explore options like Botulinum Neurotoxins and Dermal Fillers from the convenience of their homes. Let's delve into the world of virtual consultations and how they are reshaping the client experience.

The Digital Consultation Experience

Virtual consultations harness the power of video conferencing tools, secure messaging apps, and specialized telemedicine platforms to connect Clients with aesthetic professionals. These technologies not only enable face-to-face interactions but also facilitate the secure sharing of images, medical histories, and treatment plans.

The Botulinum Neurotoxins Consultation

Botulinum Neurotoxins, popularly known as Botox, Daxxify, Dysport, and Xeomin, are sought-after for diminishing wrinkles and fine lines. Virtual consultations for these treatments follow a structured process:

· **Initial Evaluation:** Clients provide detailed medical backgrounds, past aesthetic procedures, and specific concerns. Facial expression photos may be required to assess muscle movement and skin condition.

· **Live Consultation:** Through video calls, practitioners analyze facial anatomy, discuss desired outcomes, and outline how Botulinum Neurotoxins can help achieve those goals. Client queries and worries are also addressed.

· **Tailored Treatment Plan:** Based on the assessment, a personalized treatment plan is crafted, detailing injection sites, anticipated results, and potential side effects. This plan is typically shared securely with the client for further review.

The Dermal Fillers Consultation

Dermal Fillers, utilized to restore facial volume and smoothness, also benefit from virtual consultations:

· **Initial Evaluation:** Clients share medical histories and current skin conditions via online questionnaires. Photos focusing on areas of concern, like cheeks, chin, and lips in preliminary evaluations.

- **Live Consultation:** Through video calls, practitioners analyze facial anatomy, discuss desired outcomes, and outline how Dermal Filler can help achieve those goals. Client queries and worries are also addressed. The virtual platform allows practitioners to discuss various filler options, including hyaluronic acid-based fillers (e.g., Juvederm, Restylane). Product workings, longevity variances, and pre/post-procedure expectations are explained.

- **Tailored Treatment Plan:** Based on the assessment, a personalized treatment plan is crafted, detailing injection sites, anticipated results, and potential side effects. This plan is typically shared securely with the Client for further review.

The Permanent Makeup Consultations

Permanent Makeup procedures such as Microblading, Cheek Blushing, and Lip Blushing necessitate a deep understanding of Client preferences and skin types:

· **Comprehensive Questionnaires:** Clients complete detailed forms outlining skin types, allergies, prior cosmetic procedures, and desired aesthetics. They may also upload photos of natural features and inspirational images.

· **Color and Style Consultations:** During virtual sessions, practitioners discuss color palettes, shapes, and styles that best enhance the Client's features.

· **Procedure Guidance:** The practitioner elucidates the entire process, from preparation to aftercare, addressing concerns about pain management, recovery time, and result longevity.

The digital age has brought forth a new era of accessibility and convenience in the realm of aesthetic consultations, offering Clients personalized experiences from the comfort of their homes.

4 Advantages of Virtual Consultations

1. **Convenience**: Clients now have the freedom to schedule consultations at their convenience, fitting them

seamlessly into their hectic schedules without the hassle of travel or long wait times.

2. **Comfort**: Discussing personal health concerns or aesthetic goals can feel less daunting when done in the comfort of one's own familiar environment, promoting a sense of ease and openness during the consultation.

3. **Accessibility**: Virtual consultations break down geographical barriers, allowing Clients in remote areas or those with mobility issues to access top-tier practitioners without the limitations of distance.

4. **Efficiency**: The digital nature of online consultations enables practitioners to maintain accurate and easily accessible records, streamlining the consultation process and facilitating seamless follow-ups for optimal care.

Potential Challenges to Consider

While the benefits of virtual consultations are undeniable, there are certain challenges that both clients and practitioners may encounter along the way:

1. **Technical Hurdles**: Issues such as poor internet connectivity or lack of familiarity with digital platforms can impede effective communication and hinder the overall consultation experience.

2. **Limited Physical Assessment**: Certain aspects of a physical examination, like assessing skin texture or elasticity, may prove more challenging to evaluate remotely, potentially impacting the accuracy of diagnosis or treatment plans. With these potential challenges in mind, your cosmetic injector will conduct a secondary onsite physical assessment of your skin during the client treatment

appointment to validate the accuracy of the initial prescribed treatment plan.

3.   **Building Client Trust**: Establishing a strong rapport and fostering trust through a screen can present a unique set of challenges compared to in-person interactions, requiring additional efforts to ensure a positive client-practitioner relationship.

The Future of Virtual Aesthetic Consultations

As technology continues to advance at a rapid pace, the future of virtual consultations holds exciting possibilities for the healthcare industry. Innovations in telemedicine platforms, augmented reality, and artificial intelligence are set to revolutionize the consultation experience, offering a more interactive and precise approach to client care.

Overall, online consultations have reshaped the landscape of healthcare, offering unprecedented levels of accessibility, efficiency, and personalized care to clients seeking aesthetic enhancements or medical advice. By embracing these digital tools and leveraging the power of technology, healthcare practitioners can ensure that clients feel empowered, informed, and supported on their journey toward improved health and well-being.

Chapter 9

Understanding the Benefits of Botulinum Neurotoxin Treatments

Botulinum Neurotoxins, commonly known as Botox, are powerful substances that have revolutionized the field of cosmetic and anti-aging treatments. These neurotoxins work by temporarily paralyzing the muscles in the face and neck, resulting in a smoother and more youthful appearance. In addition to their cosmetic uses, Botulinum Neurotoxins also have therapeutic benefits for muscle disorders, making them a versatile tool in the world of medicine and aesthetics.

When it comes to facial rejuvenation, Botulinum Neurotoxins are a popular choice for addressing wrinkles and fine lines on the face and neck. By targeting specific muscles that cause wrinkles, Botulinum Neurotoxins can effectively smooth out the skin and give a more youthful appearance. Advanced injection techniques have been developed to ensure precise and natural-looking results, making Botulinum Neurotoxins a safe and effective option for those looking to turn back the clock on aging.

For those interested in non-surgical neck lift procedures, Botulinum Neurotoxins can also be used to tighten and lift the skin on the neck. By targeting the muscles responsible for sagging and wrinkles in the neck area, Botulinum Neurotoxins can provide a more defined and youthful appearance without the need for invasive surgery. Combining face and neck Botulinum Neurotoxins can offer comprehensive anti-aging results, giving clients a more youthful and rejuvenated look overall.

It is important for affluent clients to understand the mechanisms behind Botulinum Neurotoxins and how they can benefit from these treatments. By harnessing the power of Botulinum Neurotoxins, clients can achieve a more youthful and refreshed appearance without the need for surgery or downtime. Whether used for cosmetic purposes or therapeutic benefits, Botulinum Neurotoxins offer a safe and effective solution for those looking to enhance their beauty and combat the signs of aging in the face and neck area.

Botulinum Neurotoxins have become a valuable tool in the world of aesthetics and anti-aging treatments. By understanding how these substances work and the various ways they can be used, clients can make informed decisions about incorporating Botox into their beauty routines. With advanced techniques and expert practitioners, Botulinum Neurotoxins can help clients achieve their desired results and unlock the power of ageless beauty in the face and neck.

History of Botulinum Neurotoxins in Cosmetic Medicine

The history of Botulinum Neurotoxins in cosmetic medicine dates back to the 1980s when it was first discovered that injecting small amounts of the toxin into specific facial muscles could temporarily paralyze them, resulting in a smoother and more youthful appearance. Initially used to treat muscle spasms and disorders, it wasn't long before doctors began to explore its cosmetic applications.

In 2002, the FDA approved the use of Botulinum Neurotoxins for the treatment of frown lines between the eyebrows, known as glabellar lines. This marked a turning point in the field of cosmetic medicine, as it opened up a whole new world of possibilities for non-invasive anti-aging treatments. Since then, the use of Botulinum Neurotoxins has become one of the most popular cosmetic procedures worldwide.

Over the years, advances in technology and technique have allowed for more precise and natural-looking results with botulinum neurotoxins. Today, practitioners are able to target specific muscles and tailor treatments to each individual's unique facial anatomy, resulting in a more personalized and effective approach to facial rejuvenation.

As the demand for non-surgical anti-aging treatments continues to rise, Botulinum Neurotoxins remain at the forefront of innovation in cosmetic medicine. With ongoing research and development, it is likely that new applications and techniques for using Botulinum Neurotoxins in the face and neck will continue to emerge, offering clients even more options for achieving ageless beauty.

Benefits of Botulinum Neurotoxins for Facial Rejuvenation

Botulinum Neurotoxins, commonly known as Botox, have become a popular treatment for facial rejuvenation among clients seeking to maintain a youthful appearance. These neurotoxins work by temporarily paralyzing the muscles in the face, which reduces the appearance of wrinkles and fine lines. One of the key benefits of using Botulinum Neurotoxins for facial rejuvenation is the quick and relatively painless nature of the treatment. Clients can typically see results within a few days of treatment, with minimal downtime required.

In addition to reducing the appearance of wrinkles and fine lines, Botulinum Neurotoxins can also be used to lift and sculpt the face. By strategically injecting the neurotoxins into specific muscles, a skilled practitioner can create a more youthful and balanced appearance. This non-surgical approach to facial rejuvenation is ideal for clients who want to avoid the risks and recovery time associated with invasive procedures.

Another benefit of using Botulinum Neurotoxins for facial rejuvenation is the long-lasting results. While the effects of the treatment are temporary, clients can enjoy smoother, more youthful-looking skin for several months before needing a touch-up. This makes Botulinum Neurotoxins a cost-effective option for clients who want to maintain their appearance without committing to more invasive procedures.

Overall, the benefits of using Botulinum Neurotoxins for facial rejuvenation are numerous. From reducing the appearance of wrinkles and fine lines to sculpting and lifting the face, these neurotoxins offer a safe and effective way to achieve a more youthful appearance. With the right practitioner and advanced techniques, clients can enjoy comprehensive anti-aging results that enhance their natural beauty.

Cosmetic Uses to Reduce the Appearance of a Gummy Smile with Botulinum Neurotoxins

Botulinum Neurotoxin injections, commonly known as Botox, provide numerous benefits when utilized in lip procedures such as the lip flip and gummy smile correction. The lip flip technique involves injecting small amounts of Botox into the muscles surrounding the upper lip, inducing a subtle relaxation that allows the lip to gently evert, resulting in the appearance of fuller, more shapely lips without adding volume. This offers individuals a natural-looking enhancement to their lips without the need for surgical interventions or dermal fillers. Botulinum Neurotoxins effectively address gummy smiles by targeting the muscles responsible for excessive lifting of the upper lip during smiling. By inhibiting these muscles, Botulinum Neurotoxins limit the upward movement of the lip, thereby reducing the visibility of gum tissue and achieving a more balanced and aesthetically pleasing smile. Moreover, Botulinum Neurotoxin treatments for the lips are highly customizable, enabling practitioners to tailor the procedure to meet each client's specific goals and preferences, whether it involves subtle lip enhancement or gummy smile correction. Additionally, the procedure is quick, minimally invasive, and associated with little to no downtime, allowing individuals to resume their normal activities immediately after treatment. The effects of Botulinum Neurotoxin injections in the lips are temporary, typically lasting several months, but can be maintained with subsequent treatments. When administered by a qualified cosmetic injector, Botulinum Neurotoxin injections for lip enhancement are considered safe, with minimal risks and common side effects such as temporary bruising, swelling, or redness at the injection site. Overall, Botulinum Neurotoxin injections offer a safe, effective, and versatile option for individuals seeking to enhance their lips and address concerns such as a gummy smile.

Cosmetic Uses of Face and Neck Botulinum Neurotoxins: Target Areas for Botulinum Neurotoxin Injections

In the world of cosmetic procedures, Botulinum Neurotoxin injections have become increasingly popular for their ability to reduce wrinkles and fine lines on the face and neck. Target areas for these injections vary depending on the desired outcome, but there are some common areas that are typically treated.

One of the most popular target areas for Botulinum Neurotoxin injections is the forehead. This area is prone to developing wrinkles and furrows as we age, and injections can help smooth out these lines for a more youthful appearance. Additionally, injections in the forehead can also help lift the eyebrows slightly, giving the face a more refreshed and rejuvenated look.

Another common target area for Botulinum Neurotoxin injections is the area around the eyes, specifically the crow's feet. These fine lines that form at the corners of the eyes can be effectively treated with injections, resulting in smoother, more youthful-looking skin. Injections in this area can also help lift the brows and open up the eyes for a brighter, more awake appearance.

The area between the eyebrows, known as the glabella, is also a popular target area for Botulinum Neurotoxin injections. This area is prone to developing deep frown lines, which can make a person appear angry or tired. Injections in the glabella can smooth out these lines, giving the face a more relaxed and approachable look.

In addition to these common target areas, Botulinum Neurotoxin injections can also be used to treat the neck. Injections in the neck can help reduce the appearance of horizontal lines, commonly referred to as "necklace lines," as well as improve the overall contour of the neck. This can help create a more youthful and defined jawline, giving the neck a smoother and more toned appearance.

Overall, Botulinum Neurotoxin injections offer a versatile and effective solution for addressing a wide range of concerns in the face and neck. By targeting specific areas with precision, these injections can help clients achieve comprehensive anti-aging results that are natural-looking and long-lasting. With advanced techniques and a skilled cosmetic injector, clients can unlock the power of Botulinum Neurotoxins for ageless beauty in the face and neck.

Achieving Natural-Looking Results with Botulinum Neurotoxins

Achieving natural-looking results with Botulinum Neurotoxins is a top priority for clients seeking ageless beauty in the face and neck. When it comes to cosmetic uses of face and neck botulinum neurotoxins, it is essential to work with a skilled and experienced injector who understands the nuances of facial anatomy and can tailor treatments to each individual's unique needs.

Anti-aging treatments using face and neck Botulinum Neurotoxins can help smooth fine lines and wrinkles, restore lost volume, and enhance overall facial harmony. By strategically targeting specific muscle groups, a skilled injector can achieve subtle yet significant improvements that look natural and effortless.

In addition to cosmetic benefits, there are therapeutic benefits of face and neck Botulinum Neurotoxins for muscle disorders such as spasms, dystonia, and TMJ. These treatments can provide relief from pain and discomfort, as well as improve overall function and quality of life for Clients suffering from these conditions.

Facial rejuvenation techniques with Botulinum Neurotoxins can help turn back the clock and restore a more youthful appearance without the need for invasive surgery. By combining face and neck Botulinum Neurotoxins for comprehensive anti-aging results, clients can achieve a more harmonious and balanced look that enhances their natural beauty.

Advanced techniques for injecting Botulinum Neurotoxins in the face and neck area can help ensure optimal results with minimal discomfort and downtime. Non-surgical neck lift procedures using Botulinum Neurotoxins can help tighten and lift sagging skin, redefine jawline contours, and create a more youthful and rejuvenated appearance. With the right combination of skill, expertise, and artistry, achieving natural-looking results with Botulinum Neurotoxins is not only possible but can also help clients look and feel their best at any age.

Common Concerns and Misconceptions About Botulinum Neurotoxins

One of the most common concerns surrounding Botulinum Neurotoxins is the fear of looking unnatural or frozen after treatment. Many people worry that their facial expressions will be compromised, leaving them with a stiff or plastic appearance. However, when administered by a skilled and experienced practitioner, Botulinum Neurotoxins can provide natural-looking results that enhance the face's beauty rather than detract from it. By targeting specific muscles responsible for wrinkles and fine lines, Botulinum Neurotoxins can soften the appearance of aging without sacrificing facial movement.

Another misconception about Botulinum Neurotoxins is that they are only suitable for older individuals seeking anti-aging treatments. In reality, Botulinum Neurotoxins can be beneficial for individuals of all ages looking to prevent the formation of wrinkles and maintain a youthful appearance. By starting treatments early, it is possible to slow down the aging process and preserve the skin's elasticity and firmness for longer. Additionally, Botulinum Neurotoxins can be used in combination with other cosmetic procedures to achieve comprehensive anti-aging results that address multiple concerns simultaneously.

Some individuals also express concerns about the safety of Botulinum Neurotoxins, fearing potential side effects or complications. While all medical procedures carry some level of risk, Botulinum Neurotoxins have been extensively studied and proven to be safe when administered by a qualified professional. By following proper injection techniques and dosages, the risk of adverse effects is minimized, and Clients can enjoy the benefits of Botulinum Neurotoxins with confidence. It is essential to consult with a knowledgeable practitioner before undergoing treatment to ensure that all safety protocols are followed.

Additionally, there is a misconception that Botulinum Neurotoxins are only effective for treating wrinkles and fine lines on the face, neglecting the neck area. However, Botulinum Neurotoxins can be used to address sagging skin, muscle bands, and other signs of aging on the neck, providing a non-surgical alternative to traditional neck lift procedures. By strategically targeting specific muscles in the neck, Botulinum Neurotoxins can create a more defined jawline, improve the appearance of the neck, and enhance overall facial harmony.

Long-Term Benefits of Regular Botulinum Neurotoxin Treatments

Regular Botulinum Neurotoxin treatments offer a wide range of long-term benefits for those seeking ageless beauty in the face and neck. One of the most significant advantages of consistent treatments is the prevention of future wrinkles and fine lines. By targeting the underlying muscles responsible for facial expressions, Botulinum Neurotoxins can help smooth out existing wrinkles and prevent new ones from forming over time. This proactive approach to anti-aging can lead to a more youthful and rejuvenated appearance that lasts for years to come.

In addition to preventing future signs of aging, regular Botulinum Neurotoxin treatments can also improve the overall texture and tone of the skin. By relaxing the muscles in the face and neck, these treatments can help reduce the appearance of pore size, acne scars, and uneven skin tone. This can result in a smoother, more even complexion that radiates a youthful glow. Clients who undergo regular treatments often find that their skin looks healthier and more vibrant than before, leading to a boost in self-confidence and self-esteem.

Another long-term benefit of regular Botulinum Neurotoxin treatments is the potential for improved muscle function in the face and neck. For clients with muscle disorders such as TMJ, bruxism, or cervical dystonia, these treatments can provide relief from pain and discomfort by relaxing the affected muscles. This can lead to an improved range of motion, reduced muscle tension, and an overall increase in comfort and mobility. By incorporating Botulinum Neurotoxins into their treatment plans, clients with muscle disorders can experience long-lasting relief and improved quality of life.

Furthermore, regular Botulinum Neurotoxin treatments can be an integral part of a comprehensive anti-aging regimen that targets both the face and neck. By combining treatments in these areas, clients can achieve a more harmonious and balanced appearance that looks natural and youthful. Botulinum Neurotoxins can be used to lift and tighten the skin in the neck area, creating a non-surgical neck lift that enhances the overall contour of the face. When combined with treatments for wrinkles and fine lines on the face, this approach can lead to comprehensive anti-aging results that rival those of surgical procedures.

Overall, the long-term benefits of regular Botulinum Neurotoxin treatments are vast and varied, making them a valuable tool for those seeking ageless beauty in the face and neck. Whether used for cosmetic purposes, anti-aging treatments, or therapeutic benefits, these treatments can provide lasting results that enhance both the physical appearance and emotional well-being of clients. By incorporating advanced techniques and personalized treatment plans, clients can achieve a more youthful, rejuvenated look that lasts for years to come.

Therapeutic Benefits of Face and Neck Botulinum Neurotoxins for Muscle Disorders: Treating Hyperactive Muscles with Botulinum Neurotoxins

As we age, our muscles can become hyperactive, leading to unwanted facial expressions and neck movements. Fortunately, Botulinum Neurotoxins offer a highly effective solution for treating hyperactive muscles in the face and neck. These neurotoxins work by blocking the signals between nerves and muscles, preventing the muscles from contracting and causing wrinkles or other unwanted movements.

One of the key benefits of using Botulinum Neurotoxins to treat hyperactive muscles is that the results are both immediate and long-lasting. Within just a few days of treatment, clients will notice a significant reduction in muscle activity, leading to a smoother, more relaxed appearance in the treated areas. These effects can last for several months, making Botulinum Neurotoxins an excellent option for maintaining a youthful and rejuvenated appearance.

In addition to their cosmetic uses, Botulinum Neurotoxins also offer therapeutic benefits for individuals with muscle disorders such as cervical dystonia or spasticity. By targeting hyperactive muscles in these conditions, Botulinum Neurotoxins can help improve mobility, reduce pain, and enhance the overall quality of life for clients. This makes them a versatile and valuable treatment option for a wide range of muscle-related issues.

When it comes to facial rejuvenation techniques, Botulinum Neurotoxins are a go-to option for many clients seeking non-surgical solutions. By strategically injecting these neurotoxins into specific facial muscles, practitioners can achieve a more balanced and harmonious appearance, reducing wrinkles and fine lines while preserving natural facial expressions. This approach allows for personalized treatment plans tailored to each client's unique anatomy and aesthetic goals.

For clients looking to address both facial and neck concerns, combining Botulinum Neurotoxins in a comprehensive treatment plan can provide even more dramatic anti-aging results. By targeting hyperactive muscles in both areas, practitioners can create a more youthful and refreshed overall appearance, enhancing the contours of the face and neck for a more harmonious and balanced look. With advanced techniques and expertise in injecting Botulinum Neurotoxins, practitioners can achieve beautiful and natural-looking results for their affluent clients seeking ageless beauty in the face and neck.

Masseter Muscle Injection: A Targeted Approach to Alleviating TMJ

Temporomandibular joint disorder (TMJ) is a complex condition characterized by pain, stiffness, and dysfunction of the jaw joint and surrounding muscles. Among the various treatment modalities available, injecting Botulinum

Neurotoxins into the masseter muscles has gained recognition as an effective therapeutic intervention for TMJ.

Understanding Masseter Muscle Dysfunction in TMJ

The masseter muscles, located on each side of the jaw, are responsible for closing the mouth and exerting force during chewing. In individuals with TMJ disorder, these muscles can become overactive or hypertonic, leading to excessive tension, pain, and jaw dysfunction. By targeting the masseter muscles with Botulinum Neurotoxin injections, cosmetic injectors can selectively reduce muscle activity and alleviate TMJ-related symptoms.

Clinical Outcomes and Efficacy

Numerous studies have demonstrated the efficacy of masseter muscle injections with Botulinum Neurotoxins in relieving TMJ-related pain and dysfunction. Clients often experience significant improvements in jaw pain, muscle tenderness, and range of motion following treatment. The effects of Botulinum Neurotoxins typically manifest within days to weeks after injection and can last for several months before requiring repeat treatment.

Avoiding Common Mistakes and Complications in Botulinum Neurotoxin Injections

In the world of cosmetic procedures, Botulinum Neurotoxin injections have become increasingly popular for their ability to reduce wrinkles and fine lines on the face and neck. However, like any medical procedure, there are common mistakes and complications that can arise if not performed correctly. To ensure the best results and avoid any unwanted side effects, it is essential to follow certain guidelines when undergoing Botulinum Neurotoxin injections.

Another mistake to avoid is over-injecting the neurotoxin, which can lead to a frozen or unnatural appearance. It is important for the practitioner to have a thorough understanding of facial anatomy and muscle movement to ensure that the injections are placed in the right areas and in the correct dosage. This will help achieve a natural and balanced look without compromising facial expressions.

Complications can arise if proper aftercare instructions are not followed. It is important to follow all post-injection guidelines provided by the practitioner. This will help reduce the risk of infection and ensure a smooth recovery process.

Avoiding common mistakes and complications in Botulinum Neurotoxin injections is essential for achieving the best results. By choosing a qualified cosmetic injector practitioner, avoiding over-injection, and following proper aftercare instructions, you can enjoy the benefits of a more youthful and rejuvenated appearance without any unwanted side effects. Remember to do your research and ask questions before undergoing any cosmetic procedure to ensure a safe and successful outcome.

Chapter 10

Facial Contouring and Volume Restoration using Dermal Fillers

In recent years, the popularity of Dermal Fillers has soared, offering a non-invasive method to revitalize and enhance various facial features. Let's explore the realm of Dermal

Fillers, with a focus on how they can elevate the lips, cheeks, and chin. Whether your goal is to achieve a subtle lip enhancement, sculpted cheekbones, or a refined chin profile without surgery, Dermal Fillers present a safe and efficient solution.

One of the standout advantages of Dermal Fillers lies in their capacity to replenish volume and definition to the lips. Lip fillers can augment volume, enhance lip borders, and address any asymmetry concerns. Through precise injections in targeted lip areas, a skilled professional can craft a natural-looking enhancement that harmonizes with your facial structure.

Cheek augmentation is another sought-after application of Dermal Fillers, especially for individuals aiming to regain a more youthful appearance. By skillfully administering fillers into the cheek area, a lifted and contoured look can be achieved, enhancing facial contours and symmetry. This technique aids in restoring lost volume and enhancing overall facial balance.

For those desiring to redefine their chin shape, Dermal Fillers offer a non-surgical route to traditional chin augmentation methods. By injecting fillers into the chin region, a more proportionate profile and defined jawline can be attained. This approach can also address chin dimples and asymmetry, leading to a more balanced facial aesthetic.

In summary, Dermal Fillers provide a versatile and efficient solution for enhancing the lips, cheeks, and chin. Whether you seek to replenish volume, refine contours, or rectify asymmetries, Dermal Fillers can assist in realizing your aesthetic aspirations. Collaborating with a proficient and seasoned practitioner ensures that you achieve natural-looking outcomes that complement your unique features.

Lip Envy with Dermal Fillers: Symmetry and Fuller Lips

Natural-looking lip enhancement is a popular procedure among clients seeking to improve the appearance of their lips without the need for surgery. Dermal Fillers are a safe and effective way to add volume to the lips, define the lip border, and create a more balanced and symmetrical look. By working with a skilled and experienced practitioner, clients can achieve natural-looking results that enhance their features while still looking like themselves.

When it comes to natural-looking lip enhancement, the key is to choose the right type of filler and placement technique. Hyaluronic acid fillers are commonly used for lip augmentation because they provide natural-looking results and can be easily adjusted or dissolved if needed. By strategically injecting filler into the lips and surrounding areas, a practitioner can create a subtle and harmonious enhancement that complements the client's facial features.

Cheekbone contouring with Dermal Fillers is another popular procedure that can enhance the overall appearance of the face. By adding volume to the cheeks, a practitioner can create a more youthful and lifted look while also improving facial symmetry. Dermal Fillers can be strategically placed along the cheekbones to enhance their shape and definition, resulting in a natural-looking enhancement that lasts for several months.

Non-surgical chin augmentation is a great option for clients looking to improve the balance and proportion of their face without undergoing surgery. By using Dermal Fillers to add volume to the chin, a practitioner can create a more defined jawline and improve the overall harmony of the facial features. This procedure can also help correct a weak or recessed chin, creating a more balanced and attractive profile.

Overall, natural-looking lip enhancement, cheekbone contouring, and non-surgical chin augmentation are all effective ways to enhance the features of the face without the need for surgery. By working with a skilled practitioner who specializes in Dermal Fillers, clients can achieve subtle and natural-looking results that enhance their appearance while still looking like themselves. It is important to choose a practitioner who has experience with these procedures and who understands the nuances of facial anatomy to ensure optimal results.

Lip Volume Restoration

Lip volume restoration is a popular procedure among clients seeking to enhance their lips for a fuller and more youthful appearance. As we age, our lips can lose volume and definition, leading to a less youthful look. Dermal Fillers are a great option for restoring lost volume in the lips, as they can help plump and define the lip area for a more youthful appearance.

During a lip volume restoration procedure, a Dermal Filler containing hyaluronic acid is injected into the lips to add volume and enhance their shape. Hyaluronic acid is a natural substance found in the body that helps to hydrate and plump the skin. By injecting this filler into the lips, clients can achieve a natural-looking enhancement that lasts for several months.

One of the benefits of lip volume restoration with Dermal Fillers is that the results are immediate, with clients noticing a difference in their lips right after the procedure. Additionally, the procedure is minimally invasive, with little to no downtime required. Clients can return to their daily activities right after the treatment, making it a convenient option for those with busy schedules.

It is important to choose a skilled and experienced practitioner for lip volume restoration with Dermal Fillers to ensure safe and natural-looking results. During the consultation, the practitioner will discuss the client's goals and expectations for the procedure, as well as any potential risks or side effects. By working closely with a qualified practitioner, clients can achieve the desired results while maintaining a natural appearance.

Overall, lip volume restoration with Dermal Fillers is a safe and effective way to enhance the lips for a fuller and more youthful look. Whether clients are looking to add volume to thin lips or restore lost volume due to aging, Dermal Fillers can help achieve a natural-looking enhancement that lasts for several months.

Lip Border Definition with Dermal Fillers

Lip border definition with Dermal Fillers is a popular procedure among individuals looking to enhance the appearance of their cupid's bow and/ or vermillion border. By strategically injecting fillers along the border of the lips, a more defined and prominent lip line can be achieved. This can create a more youthful and attractive appearance, as well as improve symmetry and balance in the overall facial features.

One of the key benefits of lip border definition with Dermal Fillers is the ability to customize the treatment to suit each individual's unique facial anatomy and desired outcome.

The filler material used is typically a hyaluronic acid-based gel, which is safe and biocompatible with the body. The procedure is minimally invasive and can be performed in a quick office visit, with minimal downtime for recovery.

When considering lip border definition with Dermal Fillers, it is important to consult with a skilled and experienced injector who specializes in lip enhancement procedures. They will be able to assess your facial features, discuss your goals and expectations, and recommend a treatment plan that is tailored to your specific needs. It is also essential to choose a reputable clinic that uses high-quality products and follows strict safety protocols.

After the procedure, you may experience some minor swelling, bruising, or redness at the injection sites. These side effects are temporary and should subside within a few days. Results from lip border definition with Dermal Fillers can last anywhere from six months to a year, depending on the type of filler used and individual factors such as metabolism and lifestyle habits.

Overall, lip border definition with Dermal Fillers is a safe and effective way to enhance the appearance of your lips and achieve a more defined and attractive lip line. With the guidance of a skilled injector and proper aftercare, you can enjoy natural-looking results that enhance your features and boost your confidence.

Cheekbone Contouring and Volumizing using Dermal Fillers

Cheekbone contouring with Dermal Fillers is a popular procedure among individuals looking to enhance their facial features without undergoing invasive surgery. Dermal Fillers offer a non-surgical solution for achieving a more defined and sculpted look in the cheekbone area. By strategically injecting fillers along the cheekbones, a skilled injector can create subtle enhancements that help to lift and contour the face.

During the cheekbone contouring procedure, a Dermal Filler containing hyaluronic acid is injected into specific areas of the cheeks to add volume and definition. The filler helps to plump up the cheeks and create a more youthful appearance by lifting the skin and smoothing out fine lines and wrinkles. The results are instant, and Clients can enjoy a more sculpted look without the downtime or recovery associated with surgical procedures.

One of the key benefits of cheekbone contouring with Dermal Fillers is the natural-looking results that can be achieved. Skilled injectors have the expertise to enhance the cheekbones in a way that complements the natural contours of the face, resulting in a subtle and harmonious appearance. By strategically placing fillers along the cheekbones, it is possible to achieve a more sculpted and defined look without looking overdone or unnatural.

Cheekbone contouring with Dermal Fillers is a versatile procedure that can be customized to suit the individual needs and preferences of each Client. Whether you are looking to add volume to the cheeks, lift sagging skin, or smooth out wrinkles, Dermal Fillers can be tailored to achieve your desired results. Additionally, the effects of cheekbone contouring with fillers can last anywhere from six months to a year, depending on the type of filler used and individual factors such as metabolism and lifestyle.

Overall, cheekbone contouring with Dermal Fillers is a safe and effective way to enhance your natural beauty and achieve a more sculpted and youthful appearance. If you are considering cheekbone contouring, be sure to consult with a qualified and experienced injector who can help you achieve the results you desire. With the right cosmetic injector and the right filler, you can enjoy natural-looking enhancements that enhance your features and boost your confidence.

Chin Shape Augmentation with Dermal Fillers

Non-surgical chin augmentation is a popular cosmetic procedure that can help enhance the overall balance and symmetry of the face. This procedure involves using Dermal Fillers to add volume and definition to the chin, creating a more sculpted and aesthetically pleasing appearance. Unlike surgical chin augmentation, which involves implants or bone reshaping, non-surgical chin augmentation is a minimally invasive procedure that requires little to no downtime.

Dermal Fillers used for non-surgical chin augmentation are typically made of hyaluronic acid, a naturally occurring substance in the body that helps hydrate and plump the skin. By strategically injecting these fillers into the chin area, a skilled practitioner can enhance the chin's shape and size, creating a more balanced profile. The results of non-surgical chin augmentation are temporary, lasting anywhere from six months to two years, depending on the type of filler used and individual factors such as metabolism and lifestyle.

One of the main benefits of non-surgical chin augmentation is the ability to achieve natural-looking results without the risks and downtime associated with surgery. Clients can see immediate improvements in their chin's appearance, with minimal swelling or bruising. Additionally, non-surgical chin augmentation is a customizable procedure, allowing

Clients to adjust the amount of filler used to achieve their desired look.

Before undergoing non-surgical chin augmentation, it is important to schedule a consultation with a qualified practitioner who specializes in Dermal Fillers. During this consultation, the practitioner will assess the Client's chin structure and discuss their goals for treatment. They will also review the risks and benefits of the procedure and create a personalized treatment plan based on the Client's unique needs.

Overall, non-surgical chin augmentation can be a safe and effective way to enhance the chin's appearance without the need for surgery. With the help of Dermal Fillers, Clients can achieve a more defined jawline and improved facial harmony, leading to a boost in confidence and self-esteem. If you are considering non-surgical chin augmentation, be sure to do your research and choose a reputable practitioner who can help you achieve your desired results.

Chin Dimple Correction with Dermal Fillers

Chin dimples, also known as cleft chins, are a unique facial feature that some people love, while others may wish to correct or minimize. If you fall into the latter category, fear not - there is a non-invasive solution that can help you achieve the look you desire. Chin dimple correction with Dermal Fillers is a safe and effective procedure that can give you a more symmetrical and defined jawline without the need for surgery.

Dermal Fillers are a versatile cosmetic treatment that can be used to enhance various facial features, including the chin. The procedure involves injecting a hyaluronic acid-based filler into the chin dimple to fill in the indentation and create a smoother, more even appearance. The results are immediate and can last anywhere from 6 to 18 months, depending on the type of filler used and individual factors such as metabolism and lifestyle.

One of the main benefits of chin dimple correction with Dermal Fillers is that it is a quick and relatively painless procedure. Most clients report feeling only a slight pinch or pressure during the injections, and any discomfort is usually minimal and temporary. There is also minimal downtime associated with the treatment, so you can resume your daily activities right away without any major restrictions.

Another advantage of using Dermal Fillers for chin dimple correction is that they provide natural-looking results. The fillers are carefully injected into the targeted area to create a subtle and balanced enhancement that complements your overall facial features. This ensures that the correction is seamless and blends seamlessly with your existing chin structure, giving you a more harmonious and attractive appearance.

If you are considering chin dimple correction with Dermal Fillers, it is important to consult with a qualified and experienced cosmetic injector who specializes in facial aesthetics. They will assess your chin dimple and facial anatomy to determine the best approach for achieving your desired results. With their expertise and skill, you can enhance your features and boost your confidence with a simple and effective cosmetic treatment.

Next Steps for Clients Interested in Dermal Fillers

Now that you have learned about the various options for enhancing your lips, cheeks, and chin with Dermal Fillers, it's time to consider your next steps in pursuing these treatments. Whether you are interested in natural-looking lip enhancement, cheekbone contouring, or non-surgical chin augmentation, there are a few key considerations to keep in mind before moving forward.

First and foremost, it is essential to schedule a consultation with a qualified and experienced cosmetic injector who specializes in Dermal Fillers for lips, cheeks, and chin. During this consultation, you will have the opportunity to discuss your desired outcomes, ask any questions you may have, and receive personalized recommendations based on your unique facial anatomy and aesthetic goals.

Once you have found a reputable cosmetic injector, it is important to carefully follow their pre-treatment instructions to ensure the best possible results. This may include avoiding certain medications or supplements that can increase the risk of bruising, as well as refraining from alcohol consumption and smoking in the days leading up to your appointment.

After your Dermal Filler treatment, it is crucial to follow your injector's post-treatment care instructions to minimize swelling, bruising, and other potential side effects. This may include avoiding strenuous exercise, applying ice packs to the treated areas, and staying hydrated to promote healing and enhance your results.

Finally, it is important to schedule follow-up appointments with your injector to monitor your progress, address any concerns, and determine if additional treatments are needed to achieve your desired outcomes. By taking these next steps for clients interested in Dermal Fillers, you can enjoy natural-looking lip enhancement, cheek plumping, and chin reshaping for a more youthful and defined appearance.

Chapter 11

What is Permanent Makeup: Eyebrows, Lip Blushing, and Cheek Blushing

Permanent Makeup, also known as cosmetic tattooing, is a popular beauty procedure that involves applying pigment to the skin to enhance features such as eyebrows, lips, and cheeks. This technique is perfect for those who want to wake up with makeup already applied or who struggle with applying traditional makeup every day. Permanent Makeup can save you time and effort in your daily beauty routine, giving you a flawless look that lasts for years.

Eyebrow Microblading is a form of Permanent Makeup that involves using a hand-held tool to create hair-like strokes in the brow area. This technique is perfect for those with sparse or overplucked eyebrows who want to achieve a natural and fuller look. Permanent Lip Blushing is another popular procedure that involves adding color to the lips to enhance their shape and fullness. This technique is perfect for those who want to achieve a natural-looking lip color that lasts all day.

Permanent Cheek Blushing is a procedure that involves adding a flush of color to the cheeks to enhance their natural beauty. This technique is perfect for those who want to achieve a youthful and radiant look without the need for daily blush application. Permanent Makeup, in general, is a great option for those who have allergies to traditional makeup products or for those who have difficulty applying makeup due to poor eyesight or mobility issues.

Ombre Eyebrow Microblading is a technique that involves creating a gradient effect in the eyebrows, with a darker color at the tail and a lighter color at the front. This technique is perfect for those who want a soft and natural-looking brow that lasts for years. Combination Eyebrow Microblading is a popular procedure that combines both microblading and microshading techniques to create a fuller and more defined brow. This technique is perfect for those who want a bold and dramatic look that lasts for years.

Lip Liner and Full Lip Blushing Permanent Makeup are all procedures that involve adding color and definition to the lips. These techniques are perfect for those who want to achieve a perfect pout without the need for daily lipstick application.

Cheekbone Enhancement Permanent Makeup and Natural Cheek Blushing are procedures that involve adding color and definition to the cheeks. These techniques are perfect for those who want to achieve a sculpted and radiant look without the need for daily blush application.

Benefits of Permanent Makeup

Permanent Makeup, also known as cosmetic tattooing and micropigmentation, offers a wide range of benefits for those looking to enhance their natural beauty without the hassle of daily makeup application can be a game changer.

One of the main benefits of Permanent Makeup is the time-saving aspect. Imagine waking up in the morning with perfectly shaped eyebrows, rosy lips, and defined cheekbones without having to spend hours in front of the mirror. With Permanent Makeup, you can cut down your morning routine significantly, giving you more time to focus on other aspects of your day.

Another benefit of Permanent Makeup is its longevity. Unlike traditional makeup that needs to be reapplied throughout the day, Permanent Makeup stays put for an extended period of time. This is especially beneficial for those with busy schedules who don't have the time to touch up their makeup constantly. Whether you're sweating at the gym or swimming in the pool, your Permanent Makeup will stay intact.

For clients who struggle with allergies or sensitive skin, Permanent Makeup can be a lifesaver. Traditional makeup products can often irritate the skin and cause allergic reactions. With Permanent Makeup, you can avoid these issues altogether and enjoy flawless makeup without any discomfort. This is particularly helpful for those in the niches of Permanent Lip Blushing and Permanent Cheek Blushing, as these areas are prone to irritation.

Permanent Makeup can also boost your confidence and self-esteem. Whether you're filling in sparse eyebrows, defining your lips, or enhancing your cheekbones, Permanent Makeup can help you feel more beautiful and put-together. With a natural-looking enhancement that complements your features, you'll feel more confident in your own skin and ready to take on the world.

Choosing the Right Permanent Makeup Practitioner

When it comes to choosing the right Permanent Makeup practitioner, it is essential to do your research and take your time to find the perfect fit for your needs. Permanent Makeup is a long-term commitment, so it is crucial to find a practitioner who is skilled, experienced, and trustworthy. Here are some tips to help you select the right Permanent Makeup artist for your desired procedure.

During your initial consultation with a Permanent Makeup practitioner, be sure to ask about their experience with the procedure you want to have done. It is important to choose a practitioner who has a proven track record of successful results in the specific area you are looking to enhance, whether it be eyebrows, lips, or cheeks. Additionally, take note of the practitioner's attention to detail, communication style, and overall professionalism during the consultation.

Before committing to a Permanent Makeup practitioner, make sure to discuss the procedure in detail, including the expected results, aftercare instructions, and any potential risks or complications. A reputable practitioner should be transparent about their process, use high-quality pigments and tools, and prioritize your safety and satisfaction above all else. If you feel comfortable and confident in their abilities, you can move forward with scheduling your Permanent Makeup appointment and enhancing your natural beauty with confidence. Remember, choosing the right Permanent Makeup artist is a personal decision, so take your time, do your homework, and trust your instincts to find the perfect fit for your needs.

Preparing for Your Permanent Makeup Procedure

Before undergoing any Permanent Makeup procedure, it is essential to properly prepare yourself both physically and mentally. This subchapter will guide you through the necessary steps to ensure a successful and satisfying experience.

In the days leading up to your procedure, it is important to take care of your skin. Avoid any harsh exfoliants or skin treatments that could irritate the skin and affect the outcome of the procedure. Keep your skin well-hydrated and moisturized to ensure a smooth application of the Permanent Makeup.

On the day of your procedure, make sure to arrive on time and well-rested. Avoid consuming alcohol or caffeine before your appointment, as this can affect the sensitivity of your skin. Dress comfortably and avoid wearing any makeup on the area where the Permanent Makeup will be applied.

During the procedure, it is important to relax and trust in the expertise of your Permanent Makeup practitioner. They will guide you through the process and ensure that you achieve the desired results. After the procedure, make sure to follow the aftercare instructions provided by your practitioner to ensure proper healing and long-lasting results. With the right preparation and care, your Permanent Makeup procedure will enhance your natural beauty and leave you feeling confident and radiant.

Understanding Eyebrow Microblading

Eyebrow microblading is a popular technique in the world of Permanent Makeup that involves using a handheld tool to create hair-like strokes on the skin, mimicking the appearance of natural eyebrow hair. This procedure is perfect for clients who want to enhance their eyebrows and achieve a fuller, more defined look. Unlike traditional eyebrow tattoos, microblading results in a more natural and realistic finish, making it a favorite among those looking for a subtle enhancement.

One of the key benefits of eyebrow microblading is its longevity. While traditional makeup needs to be reapplied daily, microblading can last anywhere from one to three years, depending on individual skin type and aftercare. This means that clients can wake up every morning with perfect brows without the hassle of filling them in with makeup. Additionally, microblading is a semi-permanent procedure, giving clients the flexibility to adapt their eyebrow shape and style as trends change over time.

Before undergoing eyebrow microblading, it is essential for clients to consult with a trained and experienced Permanent Makeup practitioner. During the consultation, the artist will assess the client's natural eyebrow shape, color, and facial features to create a customized plan that suits their individual needs and preferences. It is crucial for clients to communicate their desired outcome and any concerns they may have to ensure a successful and satisfying result.

The microblading process itself involves numbing the skin with a topical anesthetic before carefully implanting pigment into the superficial layers of the skin using a precise hand tool. The entire procedure typically takes around two hours, including time for the numbing cream to take effect and for the artist to create the desired shape and density of the eyebrows. While some clients may experience minor discomfort during the procedure, the results are well worth it, as they can enjoy beautifully defined eyebrows for months to come.

Aftercare is crucial for maintaining the longevity and appearance of microbladed eyebrows. Clients should avoid wetting their eyebrows for the first few days and refrain from picking or scratching the area to prevent infection and pigment loss. It is also essential to apply a healing balm as recommended by the practitioner to aid in the healing process and ensure optimal results. By following these aftercare instructions and attending any necessary touch-up appointments, clients can enjoy their microbladed eyebrows for years to come.

Before and Aftercare for Eyebrow Microblading

Before and aftercare for eyebrow microblading is crucial for ensuring the best results and maintaining the longevity of your beautiful new brows. Proper care before and after the procedure can make a significant difference in the healing process and the final outcome of your microblading treatment.

Before your eyebrow microblading appointment, it is important to follow some essential guidelines to prepare your skin for the procedure. Avoid using any exfoliants, retinol products, or tanning beds at least one week before your appointment. It is also recommended to avoid alcohol and caffeine the day before your treatment to reduce the risk of bleeding and swelling during the procedure.

After your eyebrow microblading treatment, it is essential to follow a strict aftercare routine to ensure proper healing and optimal results. Avoid getting your brows wet for the first 24 hours after the procedure, as moisture can interfere with the pigment settling into the skin. It is also crucial to avoid sun exposure, saunas, and swimming pools for at least two weeks to prevent premature fading of the pigment.

During the healing process, it is normal for your eyebrows to appear darker and more intense than the final result. This is because the pigment will oxidize and settle into the skin over the next few weeks. Be patient and trust the process – your brows will gradually lighten and soften to achieve the desired look.

To maintain the results of your eyebrow microblading treatment, it is essential to follow a few simple aftercare tips. Apply a thin layer of the provided aftercare ointment to your brows twice a day to keep them moisturized and promote healing. Avoid picking or scratching your brows, as this can cause scarring and premature fading of the pigment.

By following these before and aftercare guidelines for your eyebrow microblading treatment, you can ensure the best possible results and enjoy your beautiful new brows for years to come. Remember that proper care and maintenance are key to achieving long-lasting and natural-looking Permanent Makeup enhancements.

Common Mistakes to AVOID with Eyebrow Microblading

In the world of Permanent Makeup, eyebrow microblading has become a popular choice for many clients looking to enhance their natural beauty. However, there are common mistakes that clients should be aware of in order to avoid any negative outcomes.

One common mistake to avoid with eyebrow microblading is choosing the wrong color for your skin tone. It is important to work with a trained professional who can help you select a color that will complement your natural features and blend seamlessly with your existing eyebrow hair. Choosing a color that is too dark or too light can result in an unnatural appearance that is difficult to correct.

Another mistake to avoid is going to an inexperienced or unqualified technician for your microblading procedure. It is crucial to do your research and choose a practitioner who has the proper training and experience in Permanent Makeup. A poorly executed microblading procedure can result in uneven brows, excessive scarring, or even infection.

One important mistake to avoid is failing to follow the aftercare instructions provided by your technician. Proper aftercare is essential for ensuring the longevity and success of your microblading procedure. This includes avoiding excessive sweating, sun exposure, and harsh skincare products during the healing process. Failure to follow these instructions can result in premature fading or poor retention of the pigment.

Lastly, one common mistake to avoid is expecting immediate perfection with your microblading procedure. It is normal for your brows to appear darker and more intense in the days following your procedure. As the pigment heals and settles into your skin, the color will soften and fade to a more natural-looking shade. Patience is key when it comes to microblading, as it can take several weeks for your brows to fully heal and reveal their true color and shape.

Ombre Eyebrow Microblading: The Ombre Eyebrow Microblading Technique

In the world of Permanent Makeup, the Ombre Eyebrow Microblading technique has been gaining popularity among clients who want to achieve a natural, yet defined look for their eyebrows. This technique involves using a specialized microblading tool to create a soft, gradient effect that mimics the look of makeup. The result is fuller, more symmetrical brows that frame the face beautifully.

One of the key benefits of Ombre Eyebrow Microblading is its versatility. Whether you prefer a bold, statement brow or a more subtle, natural look, this technique can be customized to suit your individual style. The skilled technician will work with you to choose the perfect shape, color, and density for your brows, ensuring that the end result is exactly what you want.

Unlike traditional eyebrow tattooing, Ombre Eyebrow Microblading is semi-permanent, meaning that it will fade over time. This allows you to make changes to your brow shape or color as your preferences evolve. Additionally, the procedure is relatively painless and requires minimal downtime, making it a convenient option for those with busy lifestyles.

In addition to Ombre Eyebrow Microblading, there are other Permanent Makeup techniques available to enhance your features. From Permanent Lip Blushing to Cheekbone Enhancement Permanent Makeup, there are options to suit every client's needs and preferences. Whether you want to save time on your daily makeup routine or simply enhance your natural beauty, Permanent Makeup can help you achieve the look you desire.

Maintaining Ombre Eyebrows

Congratulations on your decision to enhance your natural beauty with ombre eyebrows! Ombre eyebrows are a popular choice for those looking to achieve a soft, natural-looking gradient effect that adds definition and depth to their brows. To ensure that your ombre eyebrows remain looking their best, it is important to follow a few simple maintenance tips.

First and foremost, it is essential to keep your ombre eyebrows clean and well-moisturized. Use a gentle cleanser to remove any dirt or oil buildup on your eyebrows, and follow up with a hydrating moisturizer to keep the skin in the brow area nourished and healthy. Avoid using harsh products or over-cleansing, as this can strip the skin of its natural oils and lead to dryness and irritation.

In addition to keeping your ombre eyebrows clean and moisturized, it is also important to protect them from the sun. Excessive sun exposure can cause the pigment in your ombre eyebrows to fade more quickly, so be sure to wear a hat or sunglasses when outdoors and apply a broad-spectrum sunscreen to the brow area daily. This will help to preserve the color and shape of your ombre eyebrows and extend the longevity of your Permanent Makeup.

Regular touch-ups are another key aspect of maintaining your ombre eyebrows. Over time, the pigment in your ombre eyebrows may fade or shift, so it is important to schedule touch-up appointments with your Permanent Makeup artist to keep them looking fresh and vibrant. Depending on your skin type and lifestyle, touch-ups may be needed every 1-2 years to maintain the desired look of your ombre eyebrows.

Finally, be sure to follow any specific aftercare instructions provided by your Permanent Makeup practitioner to ensure the best possible results. This may include avoiding certain skincare products or treatments, refraining from picking or scratching the brow area, and keeping your ombre eyebrows protected from water and sweat during the healing process. By following these tips and staying diligent with your maintenance routine, you can enjoy beautiful, long-lasting ombre eyebrows that enhance your natural beauty for years to come.

Touch-Up Procedures for Combination Eyebrows

In this subchapter, we will discuss touch-up procedures for combination eyebrows, which are a popular choice among those looking to enhance their natural beauty with Permanent Makeup. Combination eyebrows typically involve a mix of microblading and microshading techniques to create a more defined and natural-looking brow.

It is important to note that touch-up procedures are essential for maintaining the longevity and appearance of your combination eyebrows. While the initial procedure will give you the desired shape and color, touch-ups are necessary to keep your brows looking fresh and vibrant.

The frequency of touch-up procedures for combination eyebrows will vary from person to person, depending on factors such as skin type, lifestyle, and exposure to the sun. In general, it is recommended to schedule a touch-up appointment every 6 to 12 months to ensure that your brows remain looking their best.

During a touch-up procedure, your Permanent Makeup artist will assess the current state of your combination eyebrows and make any necessary adjustments to shape, color, and density. This may involve adding more strokes to sparse areas, darkening the color for a more defined look, or adjusting the shape to better complement your facial features.

Overall, touch-up procedures for combination eyebrows are an essential part of maintaining your Permanent Makeup and ensuring that your brows continue to enhance your natural beauty. By staying on top of touch-ups and following the advice of your Permanent Makeup artist, you can enjoy long-lasting, beautiful brows that frame your face perfectly.

Lip Blushing Using Permanent Makeup:

In this subchapter, we will delve into the world of permanent lip blushing, a popular cosmetic procedure that can enhance your natural beauty and give you the perfect pout you've always dreamed of. Whether you're looking to add definition to your lips, correct asymmetry, or just want to wake up with beautifully colored lips every day, permanent lip blushing could be the solution you've been searching for.

Permanent lip blushing is a form of cosmetic tattooing that involves implanting pigment into the lips to create a long-lasting, natural-looking lip color. Unlike traditional lip makeup that needs to be reapplied throughout the day, permanent lip blushing can last for years with proper care and maintenance. The procedure is typically done using a specialized tattoo machine that allows for precise control over the placement of pigment, resulting in a beautifully defined and symmetrical lip shape.

One of the key benefits of permanent lip blushing is the ability to customize the color and shape of your lips to suit your individual preferences. Whether you prefer a subtle, natural-looking lip color or a more dramatic, statement-making shade, your Permanent Makeup practitioner can work with you to create the perfect look. Additionally, permanent lip blushing can help to enhance the overall appearance of your lips by adding fullness and definition, giving you a more youthful and attractive smile.

Before undergoing permanent lip blushing, it's important to do your research and find a reputable and experienced Permanent Makeup artist who specializes in lip procedures. During your consultation, your artist will discuss your goals and expectations for the procedure, as well as any concerns or questions you may have. They will also assess your skin tone and lip shape to determine the most flattering color and shape for your lips.

Overall, permanent lip blushing can be a game-changer for those looking to enhance their natural beauty and achieve the perfect pout. With the right practitioner and proper aftercare, you can enjoy beautiful, long-lasting lip color that complements your features and boosts your confidence.

Enhancing Your Lips with Permanent Lip Liner

Permanent lip liner is a popular procedure that can enhance the shape and fullness of your lips. Whether you are looking to define your lip line, add symmetry, or create a more youthful appearance, permanent lip liner can help you achieve the look you desire. This subchapter will explore the benefits of permanent lip liner, the procedure itself, and how to care for your lips post-treatment.

One of the main benefits of permanent lip liner is the ability to create a long-lasting and natural-looking lip shape. By carefully outlining the lips with a shade that complements your skin tone and natural lip color, you can achieve a more defined and symmetrical appearance. This can be especially helpful for those with thin or uneven lips, as permanent lip liner can create the illusion of fuller lips without the need for daily makeup application.

The procedure for permanent lip liner involves the use of a specialized tattoo machine to deposit pigment into the skin along the lip line. This process is similar to traditional tattooing, but the pigment used is specifically formulated for the delicate skin of the lips. The procedure typically takes about one to two hours to complete, and most clients report minimal discomfort during the process.

After receiving permanent lip liner, it is important to follow the aftercare instructions provided by your practitioner.

This may include avoiding certain foods and beverages, keeping the lips moisturized, and avoiding direct sunlight. It is also important to schedule a follow-up appointment with your practitioner to ensure that the pigment has healed properly and to make any necessary touch-ups.

Overall, permanent lip liner can be a great option for those looking to enhance the shape and fullness of their lips. Whether you are interested in a subtle enhancement or a more dramatic look, permanent lip liner can help you achieve the perfect pout. So, if you are considering permanent lip liner, be sure to consult with a qualified practitioner who specializes in this procedure to ensure the best results.

Lip Liner Maintenance Tips

Lip liner is a popular Permanent Makeup procedure that can enhance the shape and definition of your lips. However, like any other form of Permanent Makeup, it requires proper maintenance to ensure long-lasting results. In this subchapter, we will discuss some important tips for maintaining your lip liner to keep it looking fresh and vibrant.

First and foremost, it is essential to follow the aftercare instructions provided by your Permanent Makeup practitioner. This may include avoiding certain foods and drinks, refraining from touching or rubbing your lips, and keeping them moisturized with a recommended ointment. By following these guidelines, you can help promote proper healing and prevent any premature fading or discoloration of your lip liner.

In addition to following aftercare instructions, regular touch-ups are crucial for maintaining the longevity of your lip liner. Over time, the pigment may fade or become uneven due to factors such as sun exposure, aging, and natural exfoliation. By scheduling touch-up appointments every 1-2 years, you can ensure that your lip liner stays looking fresh and vibrant.

Another important tip for maintaining your lip liner is to protect your lips from sun exposure. Just like traditional makeup, Permanent Makeup can be affected by UV rays, which can cause fading and discoloration. To prevent this, be sure to apply a lip balm with SPF before going out in the sun and consider wearing a wide-brimmed hat for additional protection.

Finally, proper hydration is key to maintaining the color and definition of your lip liner. Dehydrated lips can cause the pigment to appear dull or uneven, so be sure to drink plenty of water and regularly moisturize your lips with a hydrating lip balm. This will help keep your lip liner looking fresh and vibrant for years to come.

By following these maintenance tips, you can ensure that your lip liner remains looking beautiful and natural. Remember to consult with your Permanent Makeup practitioner for personalized advice and recommendations based on your individual needs and preferences. With proper care and attention, your lip liner can continue to enhance your natural beauty for years to come.

What is Cheek Blushing

Cheek blushing is a popular technique in the world of Permanent Makeup that involves enhancing the natural color and shape of the cheeks. This procedure is perfect for those looking to add a subtle flush to their complexion without the need for daily makeup application. Cheek blushing can help create a youthful and healthy appearance, giving clients a natural-looking glow that lasts for years.

During a cheek blushing procedure, a skilled Permanent Makeup practitioner will carefully apply pigment to the cheeks using a specialized technique. The goal is to mimic the look of a natural blush, enhancing the client's features and complementing their skin tone. The results are subtle and long-lasting, with many clients enjoying the benefits of cheek blushing for years to come.

One of the key benefits of cheek blushing is its versatility. Whether you're looking to achieve a rosy glow or enhance your cheekbones, a skilled Permanent Makeup practitioner can tailor the procedure to meet your specific needs. Cheek blushing can be customized to match your desired intensity and color, ensuring a result that complements your unique facial features.

Like all Permanent Makeup procedures, cheek blushing requires proper aftercare to ensure optimal results. Clients should follow their artist's instructions carefully, avoiding exposure to sunlight and harsh chemicals in the days following the procedure. With proper care, cheek blushing can last for several years, providing clients with a low-maintenance way to enhance their natural beauty.

In conclusion, cheek blushing is a versatile and long-lasting option for clients looking to enhance their natural beauty. Whether you're looking for a subtle flush or a more dramatic enhancement, cheek blushing can help you achieve the look you desire. With proper care and maintenance, cheek blushing can provide years of beautiful, natural-looking results. If you're considering cheek blushing, be sure to consult with a skilled Permanent

Makeup practitioner to discuss your options and create a customized treatment plan that meets your needs.

Aftercare for Cheek Blushing Procedures

Congratulations on your decision to enhance your natural beauty with permanent cheekbone enhancements! Whether you opted for a subtle blush or a more defined contour, it's important to take proper care of your new look to ensure long-lasting results. Here are some tips on maintaining your cheekbone enhancements.

First and foremost, it's essential to follow your practitioner's aftercare instructions to the letter. This may include avoiding certain skincare products, staying out of the sun, and refraining from touching or picking at your treated area. By following these guidelines, you can help ensure that your cheekbone enhancements heal properly and last as long as possible.

In the days following your cheekbone enhancement procedure, you may experience some redness, swelling, or tenderness in the treated area. This is completely normal and should subside within a few days. To help reduce these symptoms, you can apply a cold compress or take over-the-counter pain medication as needed.

As your cheekbone enhancements heal, you may notice some fading or unevenness in the color of your blush or contour. This is also normal and is to be expected as your skin goes through the healing process. To maintain the color and shape of your cheekbone enhancements, you may need to schedule touch-up appointments with your practitioner every 1-2 years.

In addition to touch-up appointments, it's important to protect your cheekbone enhancements from fading prematurely. This means avoiding excessive sun exposure, wearing sunscreen daily, and using gentle skincare products that won't irritate or strip your treated area. By taking these precautions, you can help ensure that your cheekbone enhancements stay looking fresh and vibrant for years to come.

Overall, maintaining your cheekbone enhancements is a combination of proper aftercare, regular touch-ups, and protecting your treated area from environmental factors. By following these guidelines and working closely with your practitioner, you can enjoy beautiful, natural-looking cheekbone enhancements for years to come.

Continuing Your Permanent Makeup Journey

Congratulations on taking the first step in your Permanent Makeup journey! Now that you have experienced the beauty-enhancing benefits of procedures like eyebrow microblading, permanent lip blushing, and cheekbone enhancement Permanent Makeup, it's time to continue your journey towards enhancing your natural beauty further.

As a Permanent Makeup client, it is important to understand that upkeep and maintenance are essential for long-lasting results and vary by each individual client. Just like any other beauty treatment, Permanent Makeup requires occasional touch-ups to maintain its vibrancy and longevity. By staying committed to regular touch-up appointments, you can ensure that your eyebrows, lips, and cheeks continue to look flawless and well-defined.

In addition to touch-ups, it's crucial to follow proper aftercare instructions provided by your Permanent Makeup practitioner. This includes avoiding exposure to sunlight, refraining from using harsh skincare products, and keeping your treated areas clean and moisturized. By following these guidelines, you can prolong the lifespan of your Permanent Makeup and ensure optimal results.

Furthermore, as you continue your Permanent Makeup journey, consider exploring other procedures such as machine use permanent eyebrow options, permanent eyeliner, permanent beauty marks, and scalp micropigmentation. These advanced techniques can further enhance your features and give you a more polished and refined look.

Remember, your Permanent Makeup practitioner is there to guide you every step of the way. Don't hesitate to ask questions, voice your concerns, or seek advice on the best treatment options for your unique needs. By maintaining open communication with your practitioner and staying proactive in your aftercare routine, you can achieve stunning and long-lasting results that will leave you feeling confident and beautiful.

Conclusion

Celebrate Your Awakening Toward the Femme Fatale Metamorphosis Effect

As we reach the culmination of our exploration into the journey of the Femme Fatale Metamorphosis Effect, it is essential to pause and reflect on the transformative path we've traveled. Each step, each stumble, and each triumph has brought us closer to realizing the full extent of our inner strength, beauty, and potential.

Throughout this journey, we've delved into the depths of self-awareness, confronting the challenges and adversities that have shaped us. We've discovered that true transformation goes beyond mere external changes; it requires a profound understanding of our psyche, spirit, and desires.

Our quest for self-discovery has led us to embrace our unique qualities, celebrating the aspects of ourselves that make us authentically beautiful. From the trials of childhood bullying to the triumphs of professional achievement, we've learned to harness our experiences as catalysts for growth and empowerment.

At the heart of our metamorphosis lies a fierce determination to break free from societal norms and expectations, forging our path toward fulfillment and self-expression. We've explored the realms of spirituality, education, and personal development, seeking wisdom and insight to guide us on our journey.

As we stand on the threshold of our Femme Fatale Metamorphosis Effect transformation, let us celebrate the strength, resilience, and courage that have brought us to this moment. Let us embrace our journey with gratitude and humility, recognizing the beauty and power that reside within each of us.

In the end, our journey toward The Femme Fatale Metamorphosis Effect is not just about external beauty or societal recognition—it is about reclaiming our truth, our power, and our voice. It is about stepping into the fullness of who we are, unapologetically and fearlessly.

So, my fellow travelers, as you continue on your path toward your Femme Fatale Metamorphosis Effect, remember to honor yourself, celebrate your victories, and embrace the journey with open arms.

www.ingramcontent.com/pod-product-compliance
Lightning Source LLC
LaVergne TN
LVHW022012080426
835513LV00009B/682